The
URGENT CONNECTION

One man's pathway of perseverance to mental health recovery

P J Milne

First published by Busybird Publishing 2025

Copyright © 2025 Paul Milne

ISBN:
Paperback: 978-1-923216-88-4
Ebook: 978-1-923216-89-1

Paul Milne has asserted his right under the Copyright, Designs and Patents Act 1988 to be identified as the author of this work. The information in this book is based on the author's experiences and opinions. The publisher specifically disclaims responsibility for any adverse consequences, which may result from the use of the information contained herein. Permission to use information has been sought by the author. Any breaches will be rectified in further editions of the book.

All rights reserved. No part of this publication may be reproduced, stored in or introduced into a retrieval system, or transmitted in any form, or by any means (electronic, mechanical, photocopying, recording or otherwise) without the prior written permission of the author. Any person who does any unauthorised act in relation to this publication may be liable to criminal prosecution and civil claims for damages. Enquiries should be made through the publisher.

Cover image: Kev Howlett, Busybird Publishing

Cover design: Busybird Publishing

Layout and typesetting: Busybird Publishing

Editor: Busybird Publishing

Busybird Publishing
2/118 Para Road
Montmorency, Victoria
Australia 3094
www.busybird.com.au

Important Note to Readers

This book is for informational purposes only and is not intended as a substitute for the advice and care of your health provider. It is the story of my journey and what worked for me, therefore I share it with a desire to offer hope, inspiration and a way forward.

As with all health advice, please consult with a competent professional to make sure any changes you undertake to improve your mental or physical wellbeing are appropriate for your circumstances. The author and publisher expressly disclaim responsibility for any adverse effects that may result from the application of the information contained in this book.

To the one who inspires the world with all their heart …

Foreword

In this deeply poignant memoir, Paul courageously bares his soul, offering an unflinching look at the profound mental health toll that comes with a life in policing. With unwavering honesty, vulnerability and remarkable courage, he opens up about the harrowing experiences and internal struggles that police officers often face yet rarely discuss. Through his powerful narrative, Paul paints a raw and gripping portrait of the psychological challenges of serving the community, while also revealing the emotional weight that comes with the badge.

His story forces readers to confront the harsh realities of police work – the unspoken trauma, the moments of fear, doubt and despair – and challenges the culture of silence that too often surrounds these difficult subjects. Paul's memoir is not just a recounting of his own experiences as a ten-year veteran with the Northern Territory Police; it's a universal story of struggle, resilience and triumph. It serves as proof that recovery from mental health injuries is not only possible but highly probable with the right support and mindset.

Paul skilfully weaves together his lived experiences with academic research, adding layers of depth to his narrative and providing a broader context for the psychological impacts of policing. His ability to blend personal insight with academic knowledge makes this memoir both an intimate reflection and an important educational tool for those within and outside of policing.

Through his vulnerability, Paul exemplifies what true self-awareness looks like and demonstrates the power of openness in breaking down the stigma surrounding mental health in the police force. His ongoing contributions to raising awareness, reducing stigma, and effecting positive change within police culture are truly commendable. This memoir is not just a personal journey; it is a testament to the strength and perseverance of those who serve and protect, and a powerful call to action for better mental health support within law enforcement.

Thank you, Paul, for your unwavering commitment to change, your bravery in sharing your story, and for leading the way toward a healthier, more supportive future for our police forces. Your openness has made a lasting impact, and your work continues to inspire change in the way we view mental health in policing.

– Grant Edwards
APM, BA, MLPG

Former Commander, Australian Federal Police
and author of *The Strong Man*.

Contents

	Introduction	1
1	Compassion Fatigue	19
2	The Disconnection	37
3	Morning Sunshine	51
4	Purpose and Direction	62
5	Mind Awakening	87
6	Being a Man	103
7	Feeling the Body	116
8	Career Identity	127
9	Empathetic Leadership	139
10	For My Children	148
11	Trustworthy and Dependable	153
12	Secret Sauce	163
13	Nitty Gritty	173
14	Growing Your Tool Kit	187
	Conclusion	215
	Bibliography	225
	List of Images	231
	Testimonials	233

Introduction

Come back to the room. I was trying to visualise two things in the room: the psychologist asking me to look around and to tell them what I could see. I was there in body but my mind was somewhere else. I sat there confused and disorientated. It was like being in a Marvel movie, one image after another, continually picking up pace, colours changing, then free-falling into a black hole without the ability to stop.

I found myself in a past traumatic incident, able to walk through the scene without anyone seeing me, everything in slow motion, heart racing, breathing shallow. It felt like the room temperature suddenly dropped. Observing my breath, I saw the air coming out of my mouth like it does on a cold frosty morning, one breath followed by another. Was this in my mind or was it happening?

Trying to establish what was real and what was a memory overwhelmed me. I was no longer present but travelling through the past, gasping from guilt and shame, knowing that I could have done better trying to save people's lives.

I'm a very proud man, not because of wealth or material possessions but due to my desire to put others' wellbeing before my own. I came from humble beginnings as a young boy walking along the sea walls of a cold Scottish fishing village on the east coast. Arbroath was a town of significant history involving the independence of Scotland.

Uluru, NT: heart of our beautiful nation I fell in love with.

I had no concept of the man I would eventually become, from a place that was abundant in history to living in Australia. At the age of seven years old, I was informed by my parents that we were travelling to the other side of the world.

My father was a professional football (soccer) player, previously playing for the national team and the highest leagues in Scotland. He was offered a starting position with an Australian national league team, Footscray J.U.S.T. in Melbourne. I transformed from a frightened boy in a new land into a fearless leader, full of compassion and empathy for the people I encountered and a person who never gave up on life, no matter what obstacle or difficult experience and who wants more and still wants to give more.

I have always worked and developed skills and knowledge throughout my adult life. As a qualified tradesman, plumbing was a passion. The ability to provide a necessary service to others while navigating the pressures of life in the building industry of Melbourne was something I enjoyed and was proud of.

I loved the conversations with other tradespeople on building sites and was a social butterfly who loved going out and having fun with my friends during the week. But I became tired of the continuous travelling in heavy traffic, and bored of living in the same area. I wanted more. The need to see what else was out there and experience a different life from my friends and family was strong. In what felt like an instant, I went from being surrounded by high-rise buildings to working as a station hand on a remote Camel Farm bull-catching camels, riding quad bikes, and enjoying the vast wilderness, natural beauty and serenity of the Australian outback.

In 2004, I joined the Northern Territory Police, and it was demanding from the beginning. I was unprepared and unaware of what was about to happen, mentally and physically.

"I want 50 push-ups, or everyone will be running 5 kilometres!" WTF?! This wasn't in the brochure! I was supposed to be in high-speed chases catching criminals, with flashing lights and sirens! Learning to enjoy intense physical training every morning for six months took some time. I was then faced with studying as an adult, learning to learn again after so many years away from school. I found a new stress and had to find a way to cope. It was constant and I had an overwhelming feeling that I was drowning.

No one understood how difficult it was. I fell back into an old habit, the only way I knew how to cope with a lot of stress: let's have a beer and all your problems will go away. People take medication for a headache but there's no magical tablet that helps with emotional pain. College was stressful and I know now I didn't acknowledge my mental health.

As I continued through my career the overwhelming compassion fatigue that takes over many first responder's lives, I enjoyed blowing off some steam while participating in choir practice after a run of hectic shifts. This involved finishing work at 7 am. Everyone went together and attended the police club, breakfast BBQ, music and lots of alcohol. It was a safe environment where we could all discuss the crazy stuff we encountered during the previous week, good and bad. I felt it was a necessary part of policing to have a safe space to be open and discuss any issues.

Don't get me wrong, not everyone loved each other, some enjoyed a physical fight or two and others enjoyed some other physical horizontal activities. I was emotionally numb. Basically, my cup was getting too full, so it shut down to help me cope when flooded with big emotions. Emotional numbing can have a significant impact on mental health, leading to detachment and a lack of interest in activities. Many of my friends I worked with during my career probably felt this way but didn't want to speak up or acknowledge the retribution of career loss.

I finally threw my police cap into the air – yes I graduated, I survived! I was so proud that I achieved something so special and now had purpose and direction in my life. The camaraderie and many of the friendships built during my time at the Police, Fire and Emergency services college still last to this day.

I packed up my belongings in the barracks police accommodation into the back of my ute. I was destined for another adventure, Alice Springs. The town's population was approximately 28,000 back in 2004 and was a beautiful

New police recruits. (PFES College Darwin)

Alice Springs: a beautiful desert town by day and in recent years a dangerous place at night.

place during the day but a totally different place at night which I quickly discovered.

Alice Springs Police Station: a place of amazing people, fun times and a memory of the worst incidents in human nature.

Finally, my first day on the job started in Alice Springs. It was a day I never forgot, and which frequently still appears in my mind. It was confronting, overwhelming, unbelievable. I didn't think people could be so destructive. A request came from the day sergeant to attend an outstation near Alice Springs for a murder. I was nervous about what I would see and how I would deal with it, having never seen a dead body in my entire life.

I travelled just over 100 km west of Alice Springs and was greeted by the sergeant in charge of the community.

"Paul, jump in my vehicle and we will go together to the outstation." I was filled with apprehension while at the same time showing I had the ability to perform any task that was requested. After a short drive along the red dirt road, there were piles of rubbish. The temperature was high and the density of flies was immense. I made polite conversation with the sergeant, talking about the community and football, and then came a wake-up statement: "The body is still there outside under a blanket and the house is a crime scene so be careful where you walk".

I gulped as we arrived at a red-painted house with chain mesh fencing that was broken in several places. The wind was blowing from the west and buffalo grass gently swayed in the breeze. I opened the door of the vehicle and walked to the front door of the house. "Paul, I haven't found the murder weapon yet. It's a knife so I want you to have a look inside and see if you can find anything that may have been used."

I entered and immediately noticed blood, lots of blood, but not thick and congealed. It appeared that someone had tried to clean it up with a mop. The floors were concrete, no carpet, and rubbish and furniture were strewn across the floors and rooms.

I slowly entered the kitchen area. For a moment it felt like I was walking on designer red floors with swirl patterns in every direction, but then it hit me, this was human blood. *I'm walking on human blood.* Then for some unknown reason, I blocked it out of my mind and remembered what my orders were: find the weapon. I looked down at my feet, being careful not to stand on the big puddles of blood and water mixed together, taking short periods to look up at the surroundings.

In the first room next to the kitchen, four knives were in various positions. In the kitchen, I saw another five knives. Every room I walked into there were more knives. How could I know which one had been used? It was surreal and confusing.

Finally, I went back outside and saw the sergeant kneeling next to what appeared to be a female, half-naked. As I got closer, my heart rate quickened, my breathing became shallow, and more senses came into play. Smell, in particular … a smell that still burns my nostrils after 20 years. I was told to assist in putting her into a body bag.

"Just open it up," the sergeant stated. I looked at him and said, "I've never opened one before." The sergeant took over and fully unzipped the bag, like a sleeping bag.

"Paul, you go down to her ankles and lift her, and I'll lift from her shoulders". I slowly positioned myself near her feet, my hands sweaty and uncomfortable in the disposable gloves I was wearing. I took a deep breath (through my mouth as the stench was unbearable), then I placed my hands around her ankles. But I immediately let go with shock, not saying anything to the sergeant as I didn't want him to know how I felt. Death is cold, very cold, the first time you feel it, and it stays imprinted on your hands and mind.

I edged my hands forward again and cupped her ankles like a Lego man, gently taking her body weight and placing her into the bag. The body wasn't flimsy, lying with one arm up, legs unevenly twisted due to rigor mortis. The bag was much easier to pick up when it was fully closed. Like a robot, I helped the sergeant put her into the rear of the police cage so she could be taken back to the police station for preservation.

Driving back to the police station, I didn't comprehend the gravity of what I had just seen. There was no debriefing, no "Are you ok with what you saw? How did it make you feel?" Just nothing. I didn't know how to deal with it, and I was given no guidance. You were expected to just get on with it.

There were so many incidents and crazy experiences like this throughout my career. After dealing with so many, I lost count over the years, I blocked them out and tried to ignore them. I once viewed the world as kind and forgiving, but gradually I changed and became hardened, desensitised, numb.

As I progressed through the years, I built a reputation for being accountable, hardworking, ethical and honest. As the level of responsibility increased, my true leadership quality arose, not only in command and control but also in mentoring junior police officers' wellbeing and safety. In hindsight, however, I didn't consider my own wellbeing during these years. I was oblivious to my declining mental health; I started to withdraw, I didn't socialise as much, I was irritable, had problems sleeping, and experienced low energy.

I lost interest in things and became emotionally detached, not happy or sad, just numb about everything, everyone. The social butterfly didn't exist. I didn't like going out anymore, I didn't like talking to people anymore. All I wanted was to be left alone. So much was happening in my head but I was too embarrassed to say anything for fear of people's judgement.

At the start of 2014, my world came crashing down. The Christmas and New Year period that year was a traumatic one. The relentless tragedies I'd witnessed had taken a toll and I was left reeling. I was now the patrol sergeant in Darwin and had an amazing team of junior police members I truly respected and cared for. My patrol group never complained, they just got on with the jobs that needed attention. But for a period of six weeks, it was like every shift we were dealing with another fatality, another death that could have been prevented.

It was relentless. And when children were involved, that really got to me. Children have no concept of safety or death when accidents happen. As adults, we have a divine duty to protect them. I had a young family at the time, and I remember all too well those late mornings coming home from doing long hours of overtime just to see if my children were ok. The relief was palpable every time. I never talked about what I witnessed to my family, I just said it was another "busy one".

One night, I attended a job where an intoxicated male job was causing some problems. Listening to the radio and the air conditioner, I approached the incident location and noticed that my heart started beating a million miles an hour. I placed my hand on my chest and felt a rapid beating sensation. I had no idea what was going on but it was like I'd been running up a hill for 5 minutes. I was gasping for air and my heart was trying to jump out of my chest. I sat there in the driver's seat thinking, *I'm having a heart attack!* Then I thought, *Don't be stupid, I'm fine, snap out of it.* I took some deep breaths, and my heart rate finally slowed down to a normal pace.

I sat in my police car and waited for another unit with two other officers, then attended the job to deal with the intoxicated male. I went mobile from the location and returned to the police station. I walked inside towards my sergeant's desk, thinking *What was that all about?*, then sat down and completed my paperwork. On reflection, it was a bad run of shifts that took its toll on me with dire consequences. This was the first panic attack I had ever experienced.

And that was the last day I ever worked in the Northern Territory police.

I didn't know when I had arrived home from work that night, but my successful career was over the next day. I was supposed to go in as usual for another shift, but I simply couldn't. It was like an anchor was attached to my feet, not allowing me to move or get out of bed.

For the next few weeks, it felt like I was free-falling and no one could catch me. My dreams were vivid like a tornado, with one thought after the other being picked up, spinning out of control, catastrophising everything and losing all perspective. I was freaking out. I had never truly been scared like this in all my life.

I knew nothing about how to look after my mental health. It wasn't talked about at work or in my social circles. What was presented to me at the police college was very brief information about mental conditions in people who I may encounter on the job – nothing about my own mental health as an officer. While I continued to unravel, the stigma of having something wrong with my mind intensified.

Those within the organisation I loved and put my life on the line for every day, as well as my close friends and family, started to disconnect from my life. I remember sitting curled up in a corner on my bedroom floor, listening to the sound of torrential rain outside, staring into oblivion not knowing which direction to turn. I didn't seek help or support because I was never offered any or informed about where to find it.

I was incredibly intimidated by the idea of letting my guard down and was very unsure about how I could share my genuine emotions with others. My thoughts were like branches on a large gum tree heading in so many different directions and not being able to settle. As I sat on the cold tiled floor, my mind started to catastrophise: *What do others think? Am I defective? Weak?* There was so much shame. *I'm not good enough. What will they think about me?*

I ended up bottling up this overwhelming anger. This anger and sadness festered and consumed my mind, chewing away at this precious mental space and I became physically weaker every day. I didn't sleep properly, didn't eat or drink properly and the exhaustion of the constant battles took a toll on me, as well as on my family.

During the early stages of this breakdown, my partner and beautiful young children would have seen changes in my mood. The interactions with them were distant, and I was unable to describe how I was feeling. My body was numb but also tense and shaky, and I was not able to focus on my partner. We had been in a relationship for over 15 years and yet she had no way to understand the overwhelming feeling of loneliness that had washed over me and that I experienced every day.

I remember that after all the critical incidents attended, I'd always send an email reporting what we attended as a patrol group and looked for ways to support my team members. I had lost count of how many times I put it in a critical incident report of what we had dealt with, and when we had gone through one of the biggest downfalls that happened in my career, no one put one in for me. The response back then was a generic email stating that if you need some help, then contact an employee services number and find out what was available. Contact us if you need!

The response by many police members was to disregard the whole email. So, I remember going off on sick leave and I felt so guilty and ashamed for not being able to work. I never took sick days, my arm would have to be falling off before taking a day off. Initially, I was off for two weeks and navigated the bombardment of phone calls requesting that I come into work and drop my certificate so they could plan the roster. I had very good relationships with my peers, and I thought they would have looked out for my welfare, but that wasn't the case and it's ok now. I've travelled many paths to get where I am today, and I forgive them.

Finding the strength in the morning to get up and tell myself *Today will be better*, then my kids ran into my bedroom and jumped on me to play with them. One part of my mind wanted to make them feel wanted and that their dad loved them; the other part was scared and shaky from the loud noise and attempted to hide and mask my body's reactions. This went on for a few weeks, I was paranoid with extreme hypervigilance, there was danger everywhere and I needed to protect my children. I was exhausted, my heart was racing. I couldn't sleep.

I was crying. I didn't know why. Sitting on my bedroom floor thinking this is it, how can I turn my life around when no one understood? I never contemplated suicide or made any plans to, my children are my world and I couldn't bear to leave them and deal with their lives without a father, so that option was off the table.

I needed professional help, someone who understood. I contacted a psychologist in Darwin. After the phone call, the tornado in my head started again. The stigma of seeing a psychologist: *What if someone can see me walk in?* I eventually plucked up the courage to speak to her. The first positive decision I had made in weeks, maybe she could help me, to help me sleep or make me feel better. I was hopeful and praying that my life was not destined to disappear.

When my thoughts were spiralling out of control, I had to tell myself that I needed to re-train them, but I didn't possess the knowledge on how. I was scared about what was happening to me, including the fear of change. The bottom line is when we fear change it will take courage *to* change. This concept was challenging, frightening and overwhelming. The fear of the new can be greater than the discomfort of what we know. I had to take the risk by opening up to professional help. That was where my courage stepped in as I had nothing to lose, I was already worse off. One thing has always been consistent in my life: every time I fall, I'd get up, dust myself off and keep trying.

After a few consultations I was at a crossroads: do I keep falling or start to understand what was happening with my head? I was asked to see a GP to get a diagnosis. While driving to my appointment, the world travelled by the window. I was oblivious to all the external stimuli. All I could remember when I arrived at the clinic was leaving my home and then turning the ignition off at the clinic car park.

I had no recollection of the distance, the roads, the traffic or the people. I entered the clinic and sat down, scanning the area for threats, trying to not make eye contact with anyone, hoping no one knew me there. I heard my name called out, "Paul, Paul?" That was me, my name but I didn't comprehend at first. I followed a doctor to her room. I attempted to sit down but couldn't relax. I constantly moved my legs, crossing them, uncrossing them, tapping my foot on the floor. I was sure the doctor heard this tapping, but I couldn't control it. I must have looked like a drummer. After a discussion, the doctor said, "Paul,

I think you might have PTSD." I replied, "Post Traumatic Stress Disorder?"

I sat back deeper into my chair, hoping it would swallow me up, unsure how to feel. I had never been sick with anything and now I was slowly realising there was actually something wrong with my mind. The doctor told me it would be good to start on some medication to help with the PTSD and anxiety. I was old-fashioned and didn't like medication. I hardly took anything, rarely went to the doctors, just got on with things. But obviously, this was different. I needed something to help me. "Paul, I'll also give you a medical certificate for a couple of weeks, and then you can come see me again."

I took my script for the medication and walked to the pharmacy next door. Unsure about exactly what I was about to take, I decided to google the medication. It was eye-opening, especially the side effects. It took a lot of courage to take my medication. Every morning when I placed it in my mouth, thinking of what could happen, the unknown mind field was overwhelming. When I was diagnosed with PTSD, major depression and anxiety, I thought my life was over. Having a mental health condition diagnosis meant I was finished, with no hope for the future.

Soon after I spoke with one of my closest friends in the police force and asked him to go into work and pick up my work clothes in my locker and grab my lunch box to clean as I'd left everything there on my last shift. I put my locker keys out the front door for my friend to pick up. About an hour later I received a phone call that struck me in the heart like nothing else ever had.

"Hey mate, I've just been to the station to grab your gear out of your locker, but it's all cleaned out."

I said, "What?"

"Mate, I found your kit bag but there's nothing inside of it, no shirts hanging up, nothing."

I asked if he'd checked my kit drawer in the filing cabinet and he responded with "Yeah mate, it's totally empty." I was floored, *What the fuck was happening? I'd only been off work for three weeks.*

I then called the police station. I spoke to the roster sergeant and asked him what was going on with all my property. "Paul, all your stuff has been taken out of your locker because it belongs to the police." I cut over the top of him, "Um, I haven't left the job! I've just been sick for a couple of weeks! I've just heard that someone has removed all my gear and some of it I had purchased personally." The phone went quiet for 10 seconds, "Paul it's not like you're going to come back, is it?"

I started to feel hot and sweaty, and my heart rate began to explode. "What do you mean I'm not coming back? I have not resigned."

"Yeah, well, you need to send me your doctor's certificate so I can get the roster up to date."

I thought to myself, *What a dick* and I slammed the phone down. With all the adrenaline in my body, the world was spinning around and around, and I began crying profusely.

My thoughts again raced, "Why am I being treated like this? Doesn't anyone call to see if I'm ok? Where is my family? I've worked for this organisation for so long, never been in trouble, was highly respected, always a great friend and support to others. *Is that not worth anything?!* People once used to talk about the police force in glowing terms … how everyone had your back, how it was a brotherhood. But that feeling dissipated very quickly and I was consumed with uncontrollable sadness. I was alone.

The once-clear purpose and direction I had with the career that I loved was over. I lost my identity, my personal brand, and then I lost interest in everything – hobbies, family, friends and life. Everything was black with no light. When I was alone at home, with no sounds and no TV, I just sat with my thoughts: *When will it all end?*

I attended my next psychologist appointment and was introduced to Cognitive Behaviour Therapy (CBT). Sceptical to begin with, the therapy helped to unpack some of the cumulative trauma I had encountered during the years of policing. After a few attempts at the treatment, I felt positive that things were moving in the right direction, but my health was still declining. The therapy was very draining, and the side effects of the treatment brought up a lot of memories and nightmares, some of which I had forgotten about or hidden in the depths of my mind.

I continued my treatment, but another larger problem presented itself – my living environment. I was constantly triggered by the streets where I had once worked and the organisation that failed to support me when I needed them the most. So I needed to move my family interstate to start new lives and to begin recovery at the Psychological Trauma Recovery Service (PTRS) that was specifically for first responders. Sadly, there were limited mental health resources in the Northern Territory. The house was packed, the car filled and the long distance from north to southern Australia was covered over a few days.

I began my new recovery treatment at the PTRS in Austin Repat in Heidelberg, Victoria. To improve my recovery, I either had to increase the dose of medication that I was already taking or make a change to a different medication. I was informed by the doctors that this was due to my body's ability to metabolise the medication quickly; some medications work, and some don't.

After a few months, I was getting worse. I had several relapses of depression and was then admitted to the same recovery service inpatient program, Ward 17. What followed from those discharges was a never-ending cycle of psychologists, psychiatrists and hospitalisations. I was sick and tired of everything, including all the different types of therapies such as cognitive behavioural therapy and electroconvulsive therapy.

At some point, I started to disengage from my treatment team. Having tried so many different therapies I had lost hope and motivation. I no longer felt I could relate to therapists. Somehow, I found the resilience to keep pushing, and I started to look elsewhere for ideas and help. It was a combination of a lot of things. To be open to different holistic recovery methods gave me hope and after a few more weeks, something shifted in my mind. It is hard to explain but it was like someone raised the curtains. I thought to myself, *I don't want to feel like that again* and the road to recovery began.

In the darkness of my despair, I found the courage to seek help, to confront my demons, and to rebuild a life shattered by trauma. With each step forward, I embraced a new beginning, one that was defined by self-compassion and the pursuit of healing.

Now I've gotten that off my chest, I want to share with you how I got to where I am today. Through persistence, inspiration and resilience, I never gave up on life. My journey is to give you hope that you too can do this when required.

1

Compassion Fatigue

How did I hold in the tears for so long? Maybe it's a character flaw of mine that I'm a very compassionate person and I can empathise with people. Being a police officer was immensely rewarding but it took a toll on the body and mind. Attending scenes that involved a person passing away never affected me, or so I thought.

I was desensitised and robotic as I took command and people looked to me for guidance and direction. It was hard not to feel what was happening inside my body. I became very good at shutting down my body's emotions. I felt so heavy, like gravity was constantly drawing me towards the ground; so many emotions born out of fear that it would consume me, make me lose control.

I attended a scene on the outskirts of Darwin River for a man who had crashed his motorbike and disappeared, I drove to the location in the early hours of a night shift. It was extremely warm, and no other police units could attend due to our workload.

When I arrived, I spoke to a couple on the side of the road that located his motorbike. It was almost a full moon that morning which allowed me to more easily observe the location. Looking down to my right was a steep embankment. The ground was covered in long grass approximately ten feet tall, like a large cane field. I removed my Maglite torch from the car and noticed the motorbike lying on its side; it didn't appear damaged. The engine was cold so I thought it must have been here for a while. As I walked down the embankment, the moonlight dimmed; the only light was from the torch in my hand as I knelt down, trying to find any sign of the man or his tracks. I felt claustrophobic, surrounded by the tall grass in the dark.

Some of the grass had been flattened from what appeared to be someone's footsteps. I began walking on the flattened grass, pushing through it while it cut my arms every time I pushed tufts out of the way. I must have walked for about twenty minutes going around and around in what felt like circles. I could no longer see the headlights on my police car or be clear about which way the road was.

Then without warning, the smell of death. It was a smell that had burnt the inside of my nostrils and remains with me to this day. I felt my heart rate increase knowing that I was close to finding him. It was like being in a horror movie when the music changed in anticipation. My anxiety increased when the torchlight traced across a leg. I found him.

As I stood there observing him, a feeling of helplessness crept into my mind. He was all alone and became lost in the thick grass not able to find his way back to the road. My thoughts turned to anger, *Why didn't someone notify us earlier?* The feeling of not being able to save someone can be overwhelming. I knew it wasn't in my control, but I'm human and I couldn't help empathising with him.

Then my emotions and feelings shut down. I must be in control and must not appear to be affected by what I encountered. I spoke to police communications and informed them of the situation. I then left him in the grass pulling his jacket over his face and walked back to my car. There was nothing else I could do. I waited for the crime scene members and a traffic unit to attend and then I left. Driving off from the scene to attend the next job was my duty. That was how it was, being the sergeant. My accountability revolved around my junior members – there was no time to be accountable or compassionate towards myself.

I progressed through my career knowing that I absorbed a lot of traumatic emotions, none of them mine. I was told that I cared too much about my job. I put everyone else in front of my own mental health and wellbeing and because of this, I was susceptible to absorbing the trauma of people who I had saved, protected or lost throughout my career.

It was many years later that I discovered that I had suffered compassion fatigue and PTSD. When you're a first responder and your career is focused on saving lives, the repeated exposure to and the absorption of details of traumatic events has a massive impact. This indirect form of trauma exposure, however, differs from experiencing trauma in person.

As a police officer, I responded to many incidents throughout my career: some were good and I felt a sense of accomplishment, many others were the darker side of death and destruction.

When policing organisations are on recruitment drives, the brochures are shiny and the induction videos are of cinema quality showing the highlights of driving fast with flashing blue and red lights, chasing people and walking the streets of the community. I didn't see any warnings about possible mental health injury or compassion fatigue due to over-exposure to incidents. I guess this very real, but not so shiny, aspect of the job doesn't make for good marketing.

Car Crash Humpty Doo: the driver escaped on foot from the scene.

Car Crash Humpty Doo: amazing no one was hurt.

South of Alice Springs, 2012, before my world was turned upside down.

Many years ago, I wrote my first journal entry as a way to capture how I was feeling in that specific moment. It was a raw reflection of the weight I was carrying and the world as I saw it. Over time, and through my recovery, my perception of the world has shifted.

I recently came across one of my old journals from when I first began navigating my journey. The below entry is from 2014.

> Starting a new journal brings with it a sense of hope, a belief that maybe things have shifted since the last time I put pen to paper. Right now, things are tough, really tough. Reading the IME report hit me harder than I expected. Seeing everything laid out so clearly

made it all feel too real. I've always hoped that I could accomplish something meaningful and be remembered by my peers as a dedicated worker and a good friend. Now, it feels like I've failed.

I find myself questioning: Why can others keep doing the job, and I can't? Even the simplest tasks feel difficult again. The memories of the past are creeping back into my head, and some days, it feels like I'm getting worse instead of better. By now, I thought I'd be back at work, but I'm not and I don't know if I ever will be. I can't help but wonder if things would've been different if the police had supported me from the beginning. But they didn't. They didn't care.

Not once did they ask about my family. That still burns inside me how we were treated, how they dismissed us. Sometimes, I wish this whole ordeal could just be over so I wouldn't have to try so hard anymore.

I want to feel happier, but I'm not. It's exhausting, day in and day out, constantly battling with my own mind. It would be such a relief to sleep for a week – no dreams, just sleep. Every time I feel like I'm moving forward, something about the police pulls me back in.

I find it hard to feel anything, and it affects the people around me, which I hate. Some days, I just want to be left alone, not talk to anyone. The IME report, I knew it was coming. I understand the process, but it still hurt, and I can't seem to shake it off. I just want a good life for myself and my family, but it feels like I'm distancing myself from them, trying to protect them from all the drama. Honestly, I don't care about anything anymore.

Every day feels rushed, like there's never enough time, and that frustration just builds.

My family can be insensitive sometimes, as if they think PTSD just goes away. The last few days have been draining. I don't want to do anything. I'm tired, tired of trying, tired of hiding how I feel. I feel guilty for being so protective sometimes, but I can't help it. Maybe tomorrow's massage will help, at least for a little while.

As I flip through my journal, the dates jump out at me: 2004, a murder at Wallace Rockhole, Christmas Day in Yulara, an offender with a firearm. In 2005, searching for a man who died at Curtin Springs, a major fire in January, and then an attempted murder in February. July 2005, a cyclist killed on Larapinta Drive. November, someone grabbing my firearm at a licensed premises disturbance. Later that month, arresting a man carrying an axe in Todd Mall.

In 2007, an 11-month-old baby was run over by a car. In May, the suspicious death of a female in Tea Tree. In July, another fatal collision involving a horse on Larapinta Drive. August, searching for a man who died in the bush near Alice Springs. In January 2009, a double fatality on Ross Highway. A shooting in March on Bloomfield Street. Another murder in April at Keith Laurie flats, and another one in June in the Todd River causeway. In July, a woman was run over by a train. November, another fatal on Larapinta Drive. In February 2010, trying to rescue a man who drowned in the Todd River during the floods. Later that year, a shooting at Junction Waterhole. October brought another female fatality on the railway tracks. February

2011, performing CPR on an elderly man in Larapinta Drive.

And the list goes on. So much tragedy. So much for one mind to carry.

The truth is that this needs to be highlighted as part of what you sign up for. Although it varies depending on location, most police officers see and experience more trauma than any other profession. If I were to think about how many traumatic events I attended over my ten-year career, the numbers are shocking. On an average five-day working week, I would have attended a traumatic event at least once a day which meant 20 traumatic incidents in one month. After the ten-year mark, I would have personally attended roughly 2,400 traumatic incidents, then add the traumatic incidents I didn't attend but heard about during shift change or at the station muster room from other police members. Compare that to the average person who may encounter three traumatic incidents in their life ...

The Northern Territory is known for its relentless heat, whether it's the dry, scorching temperatures of Central Australia reaching over 50°C or the oppressive tropical humidity of Darwin where the mercury hovers around 34°C and the air is thick with 90% humidity. Some days, it felt as though the heat itself could drain the life from my body. Over time, I adjusted, but the sweltering conditions intensified certain experiences, none more memorable than the smell of death.

One particular day in the summer of 2013 is still etched in my memory, the smell from that day has never left me. I was a patrol sergeant stationed in Palmerston when I was called to a rural property south of Darwin. A man had been missing for four to five weeks, and no one knew where he had gone.

As I navigated the property, I found myself driving along a narrow, tree-covered track that felt more like a path through a tropical jungle than a driveway. The air was eerily still, broken only by the rustle of the breeze through the trees. I switched off the car's ignition, and the heat hit me like a suffocating wave as I stepped out. Instantly, I was assaulted by a pungent odour, the unmistakable stench of death, a smell I had grown accustomed to, yet never fully prepared for. Anxiety prickled at me as I steeled myself for what I knew I would find.

The property itself was strewn with broken bottles, discarded furniture and piles of rubbish. At the end of the driveway stood two large shipping containers. As I approached, the smell grew stronger, burning my nostrils and causing my stomach to churn. Flies filled the air, thickening the already oppressive atmosphere. One of the steel doors was slightly ajar, and I instinctively knew the source of the stench lay behind it. My steps slowed; my breathing became shallow as I braced myself.

Inside the container was pure darkness, so I pulled out my torch and cautiously peered in. The beam revealed a scene of disarray: tipped-over chairs and food containers scattered across the floor. But it wasn't the chaos that stopped me in my tracks, it was what I saw next. At first, my mind struggled to process what lay before me. Seconds passed before I fully grasped the horror of the scene.

The man we had been searching for was there, but he was no longer whole. Time, heat and the harsh conditions had taken their toll, but that wasn't the most disturbing part. He had shared this makeshift home with two large hunting dogs. The dogs had survived, but when food ran out, they turned to the only source of sustenance they had left. It was a gruesome, heart-wrenching reality, one I've never been able to forget.

That day was just one of many incidents that added to the weight of the traumatic events I had witnessed over my career.

Compassion Fatigue

Compassion fatigue is like burnout. The high-stress levels of viewing trauma daily, plus the long hours due to under-resourcing and the lack of morale and support in the organisation, left me empty. Burnout usually stems from having too much work or too many responsibilities but as a first responder you want to keep helping, you have to keep helping. But working in that capacity can leave you open to being overwhelmed by multiple exposures to the trauma of others.

Compassion fatigue may also look like PTSD. I was feeling physical, psychological and emotional exhaustion from attending many jobs every shift, always trying to help others but feeling helpless. I also felt powerless to change the mindlessness of people's need to harm others. I ruminated about the suffering of others and was angry towards the events or people causing the suffering. I would blame myself and have thoughts of not having done enough to help the people who were suffering. I knew this fundamentally shifted how I looked at the world.

The mostly poorly organised operational activity in policing? The debrief.

I was always under the impression that after any critical or traumatic incident a debrief would take place between the junior members and senior members of a police station.

Debriefs help identify what went right and wrong during the incident and are a good opportunity to bring together everyone involved in the response.

However, debriefs are especially important to front-line police officers because they provide an opportunity to comment on how the supervisors can better support or direct them during and after an incident. It seems commonsensical, right? But one of the biggest gripes in listening to ex-police officers was the lack of debriefs after traumatic incidents. As an organisation, I believe this process is finally improving, but there is a lot of ground still to cover.

In a masculine environment, expressing those feelings in front of colleagues is too frightening for many, so most keep those thoughts and feelings bottled up. Furthermore, there has been sufficient research (Kyron et al., 2021; Maglione et al., 2022; Stileman & Jones, 2023) to suggest that debriefs in a large group impact more on a person's wellbeing than one-on-one conversations.

Police officers and other first responders who experience compassion fatigue may exhibit a variety of symptoms including, but not limited to, lowered concentration, numbness or feelings of helplessness, irritability, lack of self-satisfaction, withdrawal, aches and pains, exhaustion, anger, or a reduced ability to feel empathy. Those affected may experience an increase in negative coping behaviours such as alcohol and drug usage. I definitely noticed a change in my attitude from how I started my career to how I ended it – I became hardened and desensitised to events towards the end of my career.

In every state and territory of this great country attrition rates in the police forces are sky high. The paper "Police Federation of Australia submission to the Employment

White Paper" highlights the current strength and attrition rates of every police force in Australia.[1] People are no longer putting up with the lack of support being offered and their mental health is becoming their number one priority. If I had the ability to return to the job I once loved, there would be no questions. I would leap at the chance. But then my thought pattern changed to, *Yes, I miss the great people I worked with and the fantastic communities but there is always the constant sticking point: Will they look after me if I need help?* I know the answer is the same answer that most first responders currently think.

As I recovered, my perception changed about the improvement in my empathy. I knew I always possessed this, it increased not because of some chemical reaction in my brain but the interaction with other people and my experiences. I had many obstacles preventing recovery. I continued to push on through adversity. Overcoming these, I looked at people and situations differently. My main fault was that I was not mentally aware of my personal health.

I was burnt out, exhausted from all the emotional pain of my career. Withdrawing from my friends and family, it felt like being sucked into a whirlpool, grasping for something or someone to save me, unable to stop the downward spiral. One of the issues that overcame me was the feeling of having no time to look after myself. I couldn't attend the gym every day which I enjoyed so much. I stopped socialising with friends because of exhaustion, and all I wanted to do was sleep. However, any sleep that I got was broken and I woke still feeling exhausted. I gave so much to everyone and had nothing left in the tank for myself.

---

[1] - Police Federation of Australia 2022, "Police Federation of Australia submission to the Employment White Paper" PFA, Canberra. https://pfa.org.au/wp-content/uploads/2023/01/20221130_PFA-Submission_Employment-White-Paper.pdf

It takes hard work and time to repair your heart and soul. I knew I had resilience inside of me, but I also had to be emotionally resilient. Having time away from my career gave me time and space to re-engage with exercise and to eat properly. I found that what I had consumed being a shift worker wasn't the best for my body, it's like putting fuel in your car that has water contamination … it works for a while then more issues arise.

December 2013 was probably the most devastating observation of horrific human behaviour; I could not fully comprehend the senseless loss of human life during that period of the year. Something should be said about why people think there is a requirement to throw the rule book out the window about values, responsibilities and personal safety.

For many years, I struggled during Christmas because it was the busiest for policing. I endured so many preventable deaths. Shift work puts an enormous strain on the human body especially when there is no time for recovery. I remember working four-day shifts from 7 am to 3 pm. Most days I might get lucky finishing around 5 pm or having to cover the evening shift due to being short-staffed, so 7 am to 11 pm and returning the following day to start again at 7 am was common.

We had a unique roster that incorporated a quick change, on the last day shift finishing at 3 pm and returning for the night shift at 11 pm. Night shifts were extremely busy (when the majority of criminal offences occurred) so I had to work another four nights after the day shifts, supposedly finishing at 7 am which was a random event. I can recall sitting in the muster room trying to type up the paperwork while struggling to keep my eyes open and finish by 11 am. My body didn't know if it was Arthur or

Martha. Occasionally, after a night shift when I was just about to leave, an all-units call comes through and I'm out the door again. Some weeks, my overtime hours outreached my rostered hours The money was great but at a cost to my body.

Finally, after the last night shift, we enjoyed our choir practice with a few drinks to wind down, returning to work after three days off for a run of five evening shifts from 3 pm to 11 pm which were always a highlight for carnage.

A busy night shift in Palmerston once more attended a motor vehicle accident where a small minivan hit a tree with two intoxicated men in the front. When I arrived, they were in a pretty bad way with both legs pinned against the dashboard and the van appeared worse for wear. I controlled the bleeding on the passenger's leg as he became more aggressive and wanted to get out of the vehicle. Luckily for him, he was so intoxicated he couldn't feel his legs, they were both compound fractures. Then St John ambulance arrived, and the fire service cut the men out. I left one unit at the location and went to the next job. Around 4:30 am, that's when fatigue really hits you, my body was drained and the next few hours dragged on.

Next, another critical job came through. It was a young child with cardiac arrest, so two units and I headed out to Girraween. I arrived at the rural block and located the front door running inside. St John ambulance was already in attendance. The house was cold due to the airconditioning, and an ambulance officer called me over to the child's bedroom. I held my breath as I walked through the doorway, my heart stopped as I looked down a saw a young boy lying on the floor: he wasn't too much older than my son. He was blue in the face and lifeless. Holding my emotions back to remain in control of the situation, which I was extremely professional at, I walked over and checked the boy's body to confirm with St John ambulance staff. I observed the cot the boy had been sleeping in was full of blankets and it appeared he had suffocated.

It was Christmas time, and the house was full of presents under the tree with decorations and photos all around the living room including the boy's picture – he was the only child. I remember walking up to the father who was standing in the other room and telling him that his son was gone.

The father began screaming and wailing uncontrollably. I didn't intervene, he needed to let it out. I can still remember his screams, him running out the back door standing next to the Hills Hoist washing line crying and punching himself. I eventually tried to console him and another male police officer took some time but I'm sure today that memory still haunts him. For many years, I wished I could have done something. You wish you could have been there quicker but you can't, and you live with that.

But what if, what it could have been? Could I have done something better? I felt guilt and shame for something that, in the end, I had no control over. But it was my job to save people, and I couldn't save this person. I always think back to that day and if we could have done something, but I now know that we couldn't have.

Unfortunately for that family, they lost their only child. I remember leaving the job in the morning after the coroner's constable arrived from the investigation section. We all drove back to the police station that morning at about 11 am. We were all exhausted and decided to have a drink after work, just sit out the back of the station and talk, to unwind and just let it out. That was always a great thing to do.

It is hard to describe what takes over your mind when your desire is to better yourself. The urgent connection with the world consumes me. As previously stated, being vulnerable to different opportunities has made my journey successful. Allowing myself to mend without pressure gave me hope.

> As a first line of defence for CF, prevention is the primary recommendation (Tjeltveit & Gottlieb, 2010). In line with this, psychologists who work with individuals exposed to trauma should continuously self-monitor for CF symptoms. Ideally the organisations they work with will provide regular education and training regarding the importance of building a self-care routine. Many clinics that provide services to traumatised populations already incorporate these elements into their sites. However, the organisation should continuously monitor the need for additional support for whom they are training.
>
> Directors and supervisors of trainees should consider workload, additional duties outside the clinic, and outside stressors on the trainees. Pre-professionals are not in a position of power and may be reluctant to advocate for needed cultural changes within institutions. Administrators should also consider implementation of rotations, access to additional benefits, and advocacy efforts as part of their roles (Tjeltveit & Gottlieb, 2010).[2]

---

2 - Paiva-Salisbury ML & Schwanz KA. "Building Compassion Fatigue Resilience: Awareness, Prevention, and Intervention for Pre-Professionals and Current Practitioners" *J Health Serv. Psychol.* 2022;48(1):39-46. doi: 10.1007/s42843-022-00054-9

To overcome compassion fatigue I had to overcome the negative thoughts about myself, stop wasting energy on anger at my treatment and ultimately tackle the fear in my head. Being able to use reflection in an honest way can be difficult. Getting in touch with myself is one of the most important steps to my recovery. Without lifestyle changes, I wouldn't be where I am today. Finding the special people in my life who could listen without judgement and be able to feel a real connection made me feel safe and loved.

Some signs of compassion fatigue that may notice in yourself or your friends.

- Blaming others
- Depression
- Getting angry all the time
- Being late for work and daily life requirements
- Abusing alcohol and drugs
- No longer seeing accomplishments or successes
- Exhausted both emotionally and physically
- Constant headaches
- Feelings of hopelessness
- Irritability
- Low self-esteem
- Poor sleep quality
- No longer feeling happy
- Ignoring the problem and continuing to increase your workload through avoidance.

I have the responsibility to myself to look after me, no one else can do it for me. Starting a daily routine for learning new things like mindfulness, meditation, reconnecting and discovery has been so important. I enjoy going for a walk but I also achieve a lot through processing my thoughts and exercising to feel better internally and externally.

Allowing myself to connect with people by having meaningful conversations each and every day helped in my recovery, showing friendliness by focusing on what was being said to me. I revitalised the importance of relationships which changes the way I look at the world and may change another person's view on their world.

I had to change my narrative and stop complaining about what happened to me. It was delaying my recovery, wasting all that energy when it could have been redirected to more positive outcomes. Some days I may forget the achievements or the changes in my thoughts. Journaling helps pinpoint my feelings and thoughts in relation to my activities each day and achieve a better understanding of what stressors are not beneficial. I continue today on what emotional and physical requirements are to feel better, I make appointments for massages, meditation and mindfulness activities. If I can't look after myself, who will? It's up to me.

2

The Disconnection

I needed peace from the suffering every day, trying to live like a normal person and not always be on high alert for the dreaded black dog tracking my every move.

Big O at Titjikala, NT: maintaining the connections over the years is important.

As I wrote my story, I struggled to really comprehend the vastness of distance I covered over the years. The constant pressure to maintain appearances for my family and friends drained my energy as I attempted to slow down the tornado spinning my thoughts out of control. My days seemed like an eternity and started like I had been hit by lightning, always tired because of the constant running in my mind during the night to escape the nightmares ... so many of them.

Research states that the average human being should get eight hours of quality sleep a night to maintain good health. For over ten years, I struggled to sleep. Some nights I was lucky to get one hour uninterrupted without a nightmare. Falling asleep was also a difficult process, for I feared drifting off, that something was waiting for me, ready to drain my life force.

I told myself every night, *Please leave me alone! Why do you continue to chase me?* The feeling of worthlessness, shame and disconnection from my reality was real. I tried to run away from the demons in my sleep. My legs ran as fast as they could but the distance never extended as they approached and reached out to grab my body. I woke up into the present world gasping for air, my heart beating uncontrollably while I reached out into the darkness trying to focus on my bedroom, eventually sitting upright and crying due to the relentless pursuit of the nightmares. That was nightmare one – after one hour of sleep, the night was still long. I knew if my eyes closed again, they would be waiting for me once more. I attempted to stay up without sleeping, turning into an insomniac. My days turned into nights while my physical presence depleted from the deprivation.

My health began to spiral downward. On one occasion driving to an appointment, I'd stop at a set of traffic lights and look out of the window to see a wrecked vehicle, the roof torn off from the impact and the lonely figure of what remained of a person slumped in the driver's seat. It felt so real, like it had just happened. My body began to feel cold as I shook in my seat, my breathing changed and suddenly

I heard a car horn getting louder and louder. I checked the mirror and I could see someone waving at me. I then looked at the crash scene, but it wasn't there; nothing was there, no accident, no person. My thoughts had travelled back to a previous accident I attended. Subconsciously, my body remembered the location. I took a few deep breaths and continued my journey. The disconnection was becoming more apparent.

I love my children immensely, so the imposter syndrome of being a good father every day while I struggled with my mental health illness was a constant battle. Kids always want attention. I was the play toy they loved hanging out with Dad playing games, swimming, riding bikes, just living the dream because I lived the nightmare. Having PTSD meant I was always in hypervigilance mode, scanning for danger (even if there was no possibility of it). So the moments I could have been enjoying with my children I missed. I had to sit with guilt every day as a result.

The connection with my emotions was no longer present. All I wanted was to feel; I wanted to scream all the pain out of my heart, but it wouldn't make a sound. In my children's younger years, the milestones ticked over: teaching them to swim, ride a bike or push themselves out of their comfort zones successfully. Most people would have jumped for joy and enjoyed every memory, but I focused on what danger was around the corner. The combination of being unwell, and not being able to enjoy activities or events for many years, created a roadblock in my recovery. I had no control over it.

I lost count over the years of the number of times I was asked if I was suicidal. *Have you thought about ending your life? Have you planned it out?* The discussion of suicide always prevailed. I felt so unworthy and ashamed that I had come to this point where people regularly asked if I would kill myself. I know now I'm one of the lucky ones and I definitely don't judge anyone who is no longer here.

On the days I was really struggling, the thoughts about how my children would feel if their dad was no longer here were unbearable. I felt I needed to be punished for it, so I did. The gym was my salvation. On mornings when I couldn't sleep, I hit the gym for a few hours, pushing myself harder and harder. Then when I felt like I hadn't done enough I went again, pushing myself to exhaustion. Looking back, it was my form of distraction from those dark thoughts. I would never leave my children with the knowledge that I left them intentionally. There had been times when it could have been so easy just to venture onto the wrong side of the road. But as gravity tried pulling me in one direction, I'm grateful for family and friends who showed strength and support to pull me in the other.

Standing in front of the mirror I saw nothing; the person who I once was was no longer staring back at me. I felt nothing. Having this mindset for so many years brought on overwhelming loneliness and disconnection. I felt there was no hope anymore for me and the world I lived in. Gradually, the disconnection from my feelings, and subsequently from family and friends, became so evident that I couldn't establish what was real and what was a nightmare anymore.

I remember working in Alice Springs on a hot sunny day. I attended an incident in the community of Ti Tree for a suspected motor vehicle accident. I started my shift at 11 pm the previous day so it was an overtime call. The money was good, so I jumped at the opportunity. I left Alice with my partner around 8 am, arriving at Ti Tree at about 10 am. I was tired but I clicked into another gear when focused on a serious job. I located an indigenous female who appeared to have passed away. Sadly, I wasn't affected by what I saw. It was just another job, I locked any feelings away that I may have had.

I investigated the scene and spoke with the local people about what had occurred. Unfortunately, I was told the complete truth. The main witness was taken away from the police station by the family without my knowledge. I was informed later that the husband had an argument with his wife so he ran her over with his car while she slept. This then required criminal investigators to attend the scene. My feelings were in check but there were empathetic thoughts running through the back of my mind for the female involved. I was told the family had taken the male for punishment according to aboriginal Lore.

I understood the culture and how things differed from Westminster law, but I still had a job to do. Eventually, after long discussions, the male was released into police custody. There was no doubt that retribution would still occur (typically without police knowledge) to the male offender's family. After 38 hours straight, I returned to Alice Springs to finish my shift. I was exhausted but still heightened after the job. I honestly couldn't understand how I felt. The default was to numb the feelings and prepare for the next shift.

But it was a lot to deal with, the vast distance between adequate resources was a constant obstacle in the Northern Territory led to fatigue. Some people stopped answering call-outs so others were left to carry the load.

The sense of isolation grew throughout the years. I couldn't disclose to my family what occurred each day. I would just say that I had a "busy shift" and that "not much really happened", but something always happened. Always.

My values and character never changed. It was the constant situational numbness to everything that was worrying. Throughout my journey of recovery and personal growth, I reached a point when I began to develop a deep sense of awareness that something wasn't quite right. When I had my first panic attack, it was an awakening ... a sign from my body that I could no longer operate at the optimum level which it had done for such a long period.

As a first responder, I always worked in high-stress situations, making critical decisions that often literally had a life-or-death impact. The constant heavy workload, no respite from the continuous onslaught of tasks and responsibilities, and performing my duty often without adequate resources, ultimately took its toll. Speaking about it now, I often compare myself to a motor vehicle: before a shift, I fill the vehicle up with fuel and immediately hit 100 km/h with no warm-up phase. I hit the accelerator and went.

A standard rostered shift was eight hours most days, but I was lucky to finish after 14 hours. That vehicle continuously worked at high revs and peak power with no stopping, and it slowly wore me down past the point of exhaustion. This began to damage the vehicle internally. Like most people when they hear a noise from the engine, they'd ignore it hoping it would go away. Unfortunately, I ignored the warning signs of my internal engine for too long and my mind gave up. I could no longer identify the thoughts and feelings in my body. This feeling of disconnection began an intense journey I had no concept of.

In my experience, one of the main causes of feeling a deep lack of connection was due to not understanding how my feelings interacted with my body. I know that I was never taught how to deal with my emotions and feelings when I was younger and, as I grew older and overcommitted to things, I didn't possess the skill set to check in with myself. I just continued to focus on making other people happy while forgetting my own needs.

I didn't understand the importance of being present. I always thought about the past and the future, not spending any time in the now, and never really knowing what I wanted in life. So, my thoughts dwelled on moments when I could have done better, for example saving a person's life or when my leadership decisions weren't solid. I worried about how that would then affect my future and would ruminate over expectations and constantly not meeting them, or just hoping for it all to be over.

Connection with other people is a basic human need. I thought I was normal when I was feeling disconnected. I had to learn to be kind to myself because I was craving the connection. But the conversations or dialogue I shared with the people around me were very superficial and didn't provide any true depth. I knew that there wasn't a safe space for emotions to come out. I think I underestimated the power of connection with myself. I forgot the most important connection of all: the one with myself. If I didn't look after that lifelong relationship, how could I look after the other relationships in my life? I first needed to nurture my personal connection. This would then help my connection with others.

I deserve a meaningful deep connection, but it had to start with me. Sometimes, however, people can't provide the connection we need. I understand that just because they aren't able to, doesn't mean I'm not deserving of it. Many days I sat in my room crying because I had no ability to understand what was happening to me. It was natural to feel disconnected. I just had to remind myself to be kind and gentle with myself.

Have you ever felt like you're disconnected from yourself? It is as if you're not really living your life but just watching it from the outside. The sensation of numbness and being emotionally distant from people and activities that used to make me happy, made every day feel like I was living in thick fog, unable to focus or connect with the world around me. This wasn't the person I was or wanted to be. I experienced this type of disconnection in relation to the complex vicarious trauma throughout my policing career. In fact, I responded to the trauma in a number of ways. It changed how I viewed the world; I became more cynical, fearful and hypervigilant.

My body simply responded to the overwhelming experiences that occurred, and my mind learned to protect me from the pain and trauma. It was all a survival strategy, a state I lived in for many years, but I ultimately paid a high price for this disconnection. I was so unhappy and unable to be present, so I missed many years of trying to process recovery without really feeling or sensing it. There were times during the recovery years when feelings of loneliness crept in, and while it's normal to feel lonely from time to time, intense periods of loneliness lead to disconnection.

Moral Injury, Wellbeing, and Psychological Impacts on First Responders

Moral injury occurs when an individual experiences a violation of their core moral beliefs, either by perpetrating, witnessing or failing to prevent actions that conflict with their moral compass. This violation can lead to emotional, psychological, social and spiritual damage. The concept is gaining attention, especially in high-stress professions such as first responders and military personnel, where individuals often face situations that challenge their ethical frameworks.

The wellbeing of first responders is shaped by various factors. Key considerations include:

- **People matter survey**: Captures the emotional state and wellbeing of employees.
- **Individual feelings**: Recognising the subjective experiences of each person.
- **Bio-psycho-social model**: Understanding wellbeing through biological, psychological, and social lenses.
- **Trauma-centric approach**: Focusing on the impacts of trauma, both immediate and cumulative.
- **Secondary and tertiary wellbeing responses**: Addressing long-term mental health needs.
- **Measurement challenges**: Current tools for assessing wellbeing are often insufficient.

To address the crises, organisations must focus on valid interventions while considering the complexities involved, such as operational stressors versus content-based challenges. Historically, philosophers and veterans alike have grappled with ethical dilemmas inherent in warfare. The term "moral injury" is attributed to veterans like Camillo "Mac" Bica and Jonathan Shay who documented the traumatic after-effects of war in writings such as *Achilles in Vietnam*.

Moral injury can lead to severe distress, depression and suicidality. Beyond the individual, it can damage relationships and trust within families and communities. Healing must involve collective efforts to address the damage at the societal level.

The concept of "soul repair" has emerged, highlighting the need for spiritual and communal recovery processes. Recent studies, like one involving Minnesota firefighters, have focused on developing specific scales to assess moral injury within first responder groups. These studies link moral injury to PTSD, depression and suicidal ideation, while also identifying gaps in training related to mental health resilience.

Strategies to address moral injury include:

- **Adaptive disclosure**: A therapeutic approach where individuals discuss their traumatic experiences in a supportive environment.
- **Pastoral narrative disclosure**: A narrative-based therapy used by military chaplains to address moral injury in veterans.
- **Traumatic guilt reduction**: Focuses on reducing irrational guilt associated with traumatic experiences.

Research shows that police work presents unique psychological challenges (Violanti et al., 2017). Beyond critical incidents (CIs), operational stressors such as shift work, work-life balance and organisational bureaucracy contribute significantly to mental health issues. Understanding the interplay between trauma and operational stressors is crucial for addressing police wellness effectively.

In the military, programs led by Chaplain Lindsay Carey and others have focused on addressing moral injury among veterans. One key initiative is the *pastoral narrative disclosure* approach, which provides training for chaplains to help veterans reconcile moral injuries. This proactive approach aims to reduce the risks of suicidal behaviour linked to unresolved moral conflicts.

Reconciliation does not necessarily mean forgetting but rather working to correct the wrong and move forward. Whether in military or first responder contexts, addressing moral injury requires collective efforts to heal emotional and psychological wounds while fostering a culture of empathy and recovery.

Vicarious Trauma

Being a police officer, I often face significant occupational challenges due to my regular exposure to trauma and violence. This exposure stemmed from tasks such as listening to clients share their experiences of victimisation, reviewing disturbing case files, viewing footage of exploited people and responding to violent incidents and large-scale tragedies that involve serious injuries or loss of life. The cumulative impact of encountering these traumatic events daily can profoundly affect those in these policing and emergency services.

I had to re-learn what a man should be, redefine my masculinity and be kinder to myself. I wasn't able to disclose how I was feeling for many years because the thought of being vulnerable wasn't an option and still isn't for many men. Not being able to connect with another man in a safe, trusting and open-hearted way without judgement or fear is sadly commonplace in our society.

I now know that I want a direction to follow that is connected to my heart, and that my purpose will truly reveal itself when I continue to connect with myself, find peace, stay curious and become more open to whatever feelings or emotions show up.

I say to my friends that not every day will be perfect. Some days I may struggle, while others will be better than the previous. So, I go for a walk when it begins to overwhelm and every now and then look at my feet and take note: I'm moving forward and no longer in the same position as before; I'm constantly pushing forward. As my strength builds over time, more and more clarity and fearlessness are embodied through every cell, fibre and crevice of my being.

Succumbing to a mental health injury I once saw as a negative life experience in which I was judged, mistreated, forgotten and not supported, but I now see it as a beautiful gift to help me manoeuvre through life. I live in a deeper place of direction and meaning, protecting my values and boundaries that truly put my heart and integrity first.

For some, understanding disconnection is a difficult task. When I look back at the experiences in my previous life, I feel shame and guilt because I didn't feel the way I should have, or in the way that was expected. I'm very fortunate to have wonderful children who mean everything to me but I endured many birthday parties in camouflage so they couldn't see what was really happening with me. For most people, becoming a parent is the most exhilarating feeling in the world, yet I felt no joy or happiness, not because I didn't want to but because I was so distant from my feelings.

Some days I look back and wish for a better outcome but unfortunately, I can't change what was. My response to so much trauma caused this. The positive side is that I've spent many years trying different techniques, supports, resources and treatments to make changes that have helped me love myself for who I truly was meant to be.

I must make note here that not everyone feels disconnected in the same way. Other signs of emotional numbness may include:

- persistent low energy and motivation
- indifference toward the things or people one used to care about
- a sense that nothing really matters
- feelings detached from yourself and the things in your life
- flat affect or the inability to experience the full range of emotions
- difficulty recognising your own emotions or how some things make you feel
- a lack of facial expressions that reflect how you feel.

Like many men, it was hard to know what I was feeling. I would observe my behaviour and from there try to deduce what was going on inside me. I believe the search for knowledge and education has taught me firsthand how to better recognise, own and verbalise my feelings.

Men and women experience stress differently, often displaying distinct coping mechanisms. Research suggests that women are more likely to internalise stress, which can contribute to both physical and mental health challenges. (Pilar Matud, 2004; Verma et al., 2011; Bergen-Cico et al., 2015)

In contrast, men are more prone to externalising stress, often exhibiting it through impulsivity or aggression, while also having a greater ability to dissociate from emotional distress. Understanding these differences highlights the importance of fostering awareness, support systems, and healthy coping strategies, ensuring that individuals regardless of gender, culture, or background have the tools to navigate stress effectively.

There isn't anything wrong with being disconnected every now and then. I wanted to be present and searched for many ways to reconnect with myself, I found mindfulness was one great way to do just that. It didn't work on the first attempt but being persistent it eventually worked.

How mindfulness helps when you're feeling disconnected.

When feelings of disconnection arise, the simplest solutions are often the most powerful. Mindfulness, an ancient practice now supported by modern research, offers a profound way to reconnect with yourself. It has the potential to refresh your mind and ease feelings of isolation.

At its essence, mindfulness is the practice of being fully present focusing your attention on the here and now without judgement or distraction.

Many mindfulness techniques are specifically designed to help restore your sense of connection, both internally and with the world around you. Practices such as deep breathing, body scans, and loving-kindness meditation can be easily woven into your daily routine, offering quick moments of calm and clarity.

You don't need to be an expert to experience the benefits. Just a few minutes each day can help reduce stress and sharpen mental focus. Over time, regular practice can lead to significant, long-term improvements, including better emotional regulation, improved sleep and enhanced self-awareness. These lasting effects lay the foundation for a more balanced, connected, and fulfilling life.

The quote from James Stockdale encapsulates the balance between hope and confronting reality.

> You must never confuse faith that you will prevail in the end – which you can never afford to lose – with the discipline to confront the most brutal facts of your current reality, whatever they might be.

3

Morning Sunshine

Where are my sunglasses? It's so bright now! For such a long time all I saw was darkness, with no hope of being able to function like a normal human being again. I believe you don't truly understand what depression is until you have experienced it. There are many situations during one's lifetime in which we face overwhelming odds and nothing that we try works. The most logical solution is to give up.

During my career, I encountered many situations and events that no human being should witness. As a result, I became desensitised and hardened like a robot, so that I could keep pushing through the carnage. This choice, though, ultimately changed the way I perceived the world. I still cared about everything I wanted to achieve but after some time my cup was so full dealing with the day-to-day and I didn't possess the knowledge, the awareness or the skills to process what my mind was taking in.

As a first responder, I know now that I was particularly vulnerable to poor mental health and wellbeing. Add to that the shift work, massive workloads, increasing role expectations and the high-pressure environment I operated in, I became burnt out and vulnerable.

In addition, the culture in the police force hindered me from seeking help; I didn't know who to trust with personal information, or where to find help and I was in fear of losing my career if I spoke up about what was happening to me.

I remember the rabbit hole very well; it was never-ending as I fell into despair about what was happening to my body. On a warm, humid day in 2013, I received a diagnosis of what was going on. A mental health diagnosis is similar to a physical health diagnosis. I was asked a lot of questions, I was examined and then given a summary. When I was informed, "You have PTSD, depression and some anxiety", I was taken aback. I couldn't process the reality of what she had said. How could a doctor, after a couple of visits, label you for the rest of your life? That was what it felt like she had done. The thing about depression is that you can't see it. I wasn't crying or appearing sad in the medical clinic, it was only through the conversations with the GP about my symptoms that I was able to describe what I was going through.

I don't remember driving home that day from the medical clinic. What I do remember is that when I got home it was empty, and I walked into the bedroom, sat down on the tiled floor in the corner and cried. I cried like there was no tomorrow. I couldn't stop. I'm not sure how long I was sitting in that corner crying inconsolably, but the thought of having a diagnosis for a mental health condition was so confronting.

I found having a diagnosis, or a label, earth-shattering. Some people find it comforting as it allows them to make sense of their symptoms. But I felt guilty, ashamed and worthless. I was a strong man who thought he could do everything possible, so I felt a sense of self-blame with that label which stayed with me for a very long time. Life definitely changed for me and my family from that moment on.

A mental health diagnosis impacted how many of my work colleagues, close friends and family interacted with me. It felt like everyone I knew thought I was contagious, and they should no longer talk with me. The stigma attached to mental health was never understood until I experienced it.

So, what is depression? For me it was like everything I enjoyed, feeling happy, feeling love disappeared. When I woke up in the mornings after another night of nightmares, I was so physically and mentally exhausted I couldn't move. All I wanted to do was lay in bed and try to grab the thoughts spinning around like a tornado and comprehend them. It was difficult because of my poor concentration, I didn't understand why my brain had stopped working so I felt guilty and my self-esteem began to drop. I stopped eating properly with changes in my appetite which didn't help my energy levels, the constant feeling of being tired and wanting to try to sleep all the time.

According to the WHO:

> An estimated 3.8% of the population experience depression, including 5% of adults (4% among men and 6% among women), and 5.7% of adults older than 60 years. Approximately 280 million people in the world have depression (1). Depression is about 50% more common among women than among men. Worldwide, more than 10% of pregnant women and women who have just given birth experience depression (2). More than 700,000 people die due to suicide every year. Suicide is the fourth leading cause of death in 15–29-year-olds.[3]

---

3 - WHO, 2023, "Depressive disorder (depression)", viewed Jan 2025, https://www.who.int/news-room/fact-sheets/detail/depression

My psychologist introduced Cognitive Behaviour Therapy (CBT), which I was sceptical of at first but I eventually began to unpack some of the cumulative vicarious trauma I had. I felt positive that things were moving in the right direction. After several appointments, I still wasn't my normal self as the anxiety of attending a psychologist was difficult. CBT brought up a lot of memories and nightmares, not because I wanted them to appear but because discussing those incidents in detail puts one back in them.

There was a limit to what services and treatments were available to me. I moved my family to Victoria to start our new lives and I began recovery at a PTRS and attended a 10-week course specifically for first responders, and the medication I was taking no longer had the same effect as it once did. The people on the course were amazing, they had all been through something. I felt safe, I could sit in a room with all of them, not say a word, and people understood what was happening. That was a big change from feeling all alone. Medication was like a band-aid and masked the underlying issues. It alone wouldn't solve all my issues.

I either had to increase the same medication that I was on or change my medication. This was due to my own body's ability to metabolise the medication quickly, my health started to go downhill, and I was getting worse. I had several relapses of depression and was admitted to the same recovery service (Ward 17) due to my medication no longer working. What followed from those discharges was a never-ending cycle of psychologists, psychiatrists, and hospitalisations. I remember thinking I couldn't do it.

I was sick and tired of everything. I tried different types of therapies like cognitive behavioural therapy and Electroconvulsive therapy.

Electroconvulsive therapy (ECT) is a procedure, done under general anaesthesia, in which small electric currents are passed through the brain, intentionally triggering a brief seizure. ECT seems to cause changes in brain chemistry that can quickly reverse symptoms of certain mental health conditions.[4]

In my opinion, one of the most crucial aspects is ensuring that individuals who are prescribed ECT treatment receive sufficient information about the potential side effects. Not every intervention or treatment is suitable for every person. We are all unique with different ways of processing emotions and responding to medication. Therefore, it is unlikely that a single solution will be effective for everyone.

In 2018, I was admitted as an in-patient at Ward 17 in Austin Hospital in Victoria. My admission was prompted by the ineffectiveness of medication in managing my diagnosed PTSD, major depression and anxiety. Throughout my recovery process, I have encountered a lack of accessible mental health services for individuals dealing with these conditions.

I have been admitted to Ward 17 on four occasions, with the most recent being in 2019. It was during this time that my medical team suggested I try ECT to alleviate my depression and PTSD. At that point, I was willing to explore any potential solution, but I was unaware of the severity of the side effects. Many of the people I spoke to in the ward had experienced some form of side effects from the treatment, which could be as extreme as complete disorientation or as deeply distressing as the loss of cherished memories. Despite my willingness, I remained cautious.

---

4 - Mayo Clinic, May 2024, "Electroconvulsive therapy (ECT)", viewed Jan 2025, https://www.mayoclinic.org/tests-procedures/electroconvulsive-therapy/about/pac-20393894

I was scheduled for 22 voluntary ECT treatments and had to sign a waiver as expected. I distinctly remember that, on the days of the treatments, we were instructed not to eat in the morning to avoid any potential choking hazards. We were also given standard information about general anaesthesia. We would then travel by bus to the ECT treatment ward, situated on the other side of the hospital, and wait for our designated times on gurneys in the waiting area.

The experience was terrifying, and my anxiety soared. I have no recollection of the actual treatment itself, but my jaw was incredibly sore afterwards, as though I had been struck in the face by something or someone. This treatment frightened me to the point where I have spoken about it at Beyond Blue events, and I have never felt such fear before.

When I woke up, I was disoriented and had no idea where I was. I tried to recall what had happened prior to the treatment, but it was a complete blank. I was informed that memory tests were conducted after awakening from the anaesthesia, including questions about my name, the day, and counting. I was unable to perform any of these tasks. As someone accustomed to processing complex information, this experience was both frustrating and concerning. I couldn't even remember if I had children. I can only imagine how overwhelming and challenging this would be for anyone facing similar difficulties, regardless of their background or experience.

Memory loss was the side effect that caused the most concern among individuals. After sleeping for 12 hours, I woke up in my ward bedroom with no recollection of how I had arrived there, whether I had walked or how I had gotten into bed. The staff in the ward were supportive, and when I asked them what had happened, they informed me that I had taken the bus back, walked into my room and they tucked me into bed. Some people remembered the treatment and were able to resume their normal activities immediately afterwards.

Despite the memory loss, I decided to give ECT another try, thinking that the side effects might be a one-time occurrence. Unfortunately, the same outcome occurred. It became clear to me that the memory loss outweighed any potential benefits the treatment might provide. It was incredibly frustrating and upsetting to not be able to recall important periods of my life. Eventually, my memories did return after a few days or with reminders, but the initial loss was distressing.

At that point, I made the difficult decision to stop the ECT treatments. It took months for my short-term memory to fully function again, and I'm grateful that it eventually did. I'm aware that some people experience long-term memory loss because of ECT, and I believe that being informed about past events that one was involved in but cannot remember can lead to further mental health issues.

I acknowledge that ECT can be effective for some individuals, but it's important to recognise that it is not suitable for everyone. I'm grateful that I had the agency to make the decision to discontinue the treatment, as I understand that others may not have the same opportunity or understanding of the potential side effects.

I don't think it was one treatment alone that changed my pathway to recovery, it was a combination of a lot of things. I was prescribed a treatment of Transcranial Magnetic Stimulation (TMS), which I was concerned about, not because of the procedures or appointments, but my knowledge of what it was and the benefits.

> Transcranial Magnetic Stimulation (TMS) is a mild form of brain stimulation that uses magnetic fields generated by a simple coil placed on the head to stimulate a small area on the surface of the brain. The treatment is normally well-tolerated and has been shown to be effective for treatment-resistant depression.[5]

So, I jumped in the deep end, *What else could I lose?* I drove to Epworth in Camberwell and walked into a room but the TV was much bigger. The technicians were always nice. I sat on the edge of the bed, and he approached me holding a whiteboard marker. He then placed a small measuring tape on top of my head and measured the distance from two points according to the doctor's request. A machine was then placed above my head. Twenty treatments later I thought nothing had happened, as it was just some tapping on my head that annoyed me for an hour at each appointment.

I returned home after the last appointment, then two weeks later something shifted. It's hard to explain but it was like someone raised the curtains on the windows. I remember waking up and wanting to actually get up. It had been so long since I'd had that sensation. I thought to myself, *I don't want to ever feel that low again*, so I started measuring my progress in inches, not even baby steps!

Every day I would feel a little better because I had accomplished something else. From getting dressed one morning, to the following day getting dressed and having breakfast. The key was to celebrate the small triumphs as they added up. I started exercising more. It was such an amazing feeling getting back into the gym. It's a place

---

5 - Black Dog Institute, "Transcranial Magnetic Stimulation (TMS) treatment for depression", viewed Jan 2025, https://www.blackdoginstitute.org.au/research-centres/neuromodulation-research-centre/transcranial-magnetic-stimulation-tms/

where I always switch off from the world even if just for an hour. My diet began to improve and I learned muscle relaxation, mindfulness and meditation, and I practised light meditation with chakras. The main thing is my heart was starting to heal. I felt better about the prospects of life and still had something to give. I wasn't cured but I was in a better headspace to put coping measures in place for myself.

Mental health stigma is a significant barrier that has prevented me from seeking the necessary support and treatment for my mental health issues. In Australia, a police officer, like firefighters and paramedics, face unique challenges that can have a detrimental impact on their mental wellbeing. I believe it's important to address mental health stigma among first responders. It is crucial to implement the best practices that promote awareness, education, and support which I require to progress my journey.

I tried for many years to navigate or determine best practices and understand their importance in creating a supportive environment for me. Over the past 10 years, I have witnessed a lot of conversations regarding mental health. We still have a major issue, acknowledgement of the fact that a first responder is more likely to be injured from mental health due to the nature of the work. I sit here today feeling very lucky that I found resilience in overcoming adversity, many obstacles, and the lack of empathy from many people. I've continued to push myself to be a better person and find hope again.

I was told from the first day of my career that communication is my strongest weapon, use it well to get myself out of trouble and to acquire the necessary knowledge and skill to grow. Over the past five years, promoting mental health awareness has been one of the best practices for advocating mental health stigma among first responders.

I hope through my positive conversations without judgement can gain a better understanding of mental health conditions, reduce misconceptions, and challenge stigmatising attitudes, education, and training on mental health for first responders. I am aware there are many gaps in how I was protected and supported with a mental health injury. I truly believe in educating more about what makes the person you are and learning about common mental health conditions, their symptoms, and available treatment options.

There are many courses available especially mental health first aid training programs. I wish I had received this training when I was a recruit in college. I would have been equipped with the knowledge and skills to identify and address mental health issues, both for myself and my colleagues. I would like to establish Clinical Peer Support Programs which could play a crucial role in addressing mental health stigma. Some organisations in the private sector have these programs which can be transferred to support the first responder community.

Peer support programs provide a safe space for first responders to share their experiences, seek advice and offer emotional support. By fostering a sense of camaraderie and understanding, these programs help reduce stigma and encourage help-seeking behaviours.

It is essential to have comprehensive mental health policies and procedures in place. These policies should ensure that first responders have access to the necessary resources support, and treatment options. They should also emphasise the importance of early intervention and destigmatise seeking help. By implementing clear policies that are culturally appropriate, organisations can create an environment that prioritises mental wellbeing and supports those who may be experiencing challenges.

Collaborating with mental health professionals and between first responder organisations is crucial for addressing mental health stigma effectively. By establishing partnerships, first responders can access specialised mental health services and receive the support they need. Mental health professionals can guide, assess, and treat first responders, helping them navigate their mental health challenges. This collaboration also helps to normalise seeking professional help and reduces the stigma associated with mental health care.

Addressing mental health stigma among first responders in Australia is a complex but necessary task, including promoting mental health awareness, providing education and training, establishing clinical peer support programs, implementing mental health policies, and collaborating with mental health professionals.

We can create a supportive environment that encourages first responders to seek help without fear or judgement. It is essential to prioritise the mental wellbeing of these individuals who dedicate their lives to protecting and serving the community.

I always knew I was resilient, I just forgot where I put it. I learned about Buddhism and spirituality healing the body from a more holistic approach.

It was only the beginning, but I was now on the right path.

4

Purpose and Direction

Hi Google, what's my purpose and direction?

If only it was that simple.

For many years after being diagnosed with PTSD, major depression and anxiety I lost all direction of where I was heading in my life. Ruminating about what may have been, the void created by no longer being in the police force was overwhelming at times. I found myself feeling unfulfilled – missing the one activity I really loved: helping people. I had to consider what my purpose was in life from that moment forward.

I had been on autopilot in my career, feeling bulletproof. I placed boundaries around my mind and body for protection which ultimately failed because I never truly understood the importance of looking after my mental health. I didn't take the time or effort to even foresee the possibilities. All my effort was directed at my career. After six months of not being at work, the thoughts of being no longer remembered crept in.

I went from being around people every day, where I knew my purpose and I was passionate about the work I did, to being isolated from the people and community I loved. I felt all alone in the world. I lost my direction and purpose, my energy levels were depleted and the passion and excitement for the future was no more.

I had a lot of time to survey the thoughts travelling through my mind. What was my life's purpose now? Being depressed was demanding. The internal resilience I possessed inside was always telling me, *You can do this, this time will pass in my life, you are strong, don't give up.*

I knew that having a firm sense of purpose would prevent the feeling of loneliness and get me back involved in life. I needed this to work. My children were my focus. I love them so much and wanted to set the best example for them regarding overcoming adversity, but I was raising a family during the most difficult time in my life. I wanted to create a legacy that would help them and others to overcome similar challenges.

> The best day of your life is the one on which you decide your life is your own. No apologies or excuses. No one to lean on, rely on, or blame. The gift is yours – it is an amazing journey – and you alone are responsible for the quality of it. This is the day your life really begins.
>
> **– Bob Moawad**

At first, I felt discouraged about finding a new purpose. It was mentally taxing, but I had to look internally to find the answers. Before I could find my purpose, I had to ask myself, *What values do I have and what do I value in my life?* When I looked at my values and beliefs they had never changed. Even though I went through so much I was still guided by them.

Losing my identity was a terrible stage in my life, no direction and no purpose.

I think everyone should stand in front of a mirror at home and think about, then say out loud what their values are. It was very empowering to stand there and look at myself. Be kind, don't overthink. I stood one morning looking at myself thinking about my values: the importance of honesty, integrity, kindness, gratitude, empathy, generosity, respect, family values and so on. I had to ask myself what the most meaningful moments in life were and the reasons why. Analysing specific moments throughout my life, my accomplishments, when I felt the happiest and the least satisfied. I lost count of the number of hours I spent self-reflecting on previous emotions, on what I really care about and made me who I am today.

Change is hard especially when you have no idea about the direction you are heading. Remaining grounded in the present was the key. If I projected too far into the future, I began to feel that it was unattainable.

The fear of being rejected, not good enough and damaged were barriers I had to overcome. I had to be realistic. Because of a lack of clarity, I was inclined to avoid sharing my feelings, fearing that I would be misunderstood. This caused me to isolate myself and bury myself deeper into my thoughts. Doing it alone was difficult. I needed to have conversations with people in my inner circle who knew me the best to help highlight what my passions were even if it meant being vulnerable.

Exploring my true identity and improving my self-awareness gathered pace on my journey of self-discovery. I was mindful that I had to acknowledge and accept what I couldn't change or control and engage my energies in things which can give me a sense of effectiveness in life.

To look after myself was a big obstacle. Instead of beating myself up for all the setbacks, I practised gratitude and self-acceptance that things happen for a reason. I was my own worst enemy, compassionate about everyone else, forgetting myself in the process. For many, practising self-compassion is uncomfortable and a foreign idea but it allowed me to develop a greater sense of self-awareness on what I needed. If I could provide any advice for people, never stop learning, never stop experiencing different things in life, and stay curious about the world. I don't want to ever be stagnant; I want to always move forward.

Finding new purpose and direction, always moving forward.

Health and wellness must be approached holistically. It took me years to truly understand this, and my hope is that by reading this, you can grasp the importance of caring for the whole body and mind. We each have the power to make an impact, not just on ourselves but on the world around us. Waking up in the morning and stepping into the natural sunlight is like a jolt to the system. Your body instantly knows it's time to move. Some days are harder than others and for a long time, I struggled, telling myself I wasn't motivated or disciplined enough to improve. But the key is consistency and finding the mental strength to push through.

When it came down to the fundamentals, I had to ask myself how could I feel worthy of achieving the health and wellness I wanted. For a long time, I didn't feel worthy of pursuing it or deserving of it. As a result, I unknowingly sabotaged myself.

There's one important question you need to ask yourself: *Do I feel worthy?* I had to confront this, realising that in order to act on the advice and support from friends, family and professionals, I needed to first feel worthy of making those changes. Without shifting my mindset to one that was open and vulnerable, I wouldn't succeed, no matter how much discipline or motivation I had.

Discipline itself wasn't the hard part. Mental barriers might tell me it was easier to oversleep or skip the gym, but discipline was something that could be practised. But without that foundation of worthiness, even the strongest discipline won't lead to lasting change.

Motivation is important, but who really waits for motivation to take action? Hardly anyone. What truly matters is addressing the sense of worthiness before making any significant changes. This is crucial because it often comes down to the narrative I tell myself daily. How do I interpret my environment? Do I see everything as overwhelming and feel unworthy of taking action to break free from that cycle of stress?

I'm sure many people, like me, become self-critical about body image, how others perceive them, or even struggle with imposter syndrome. I often asked myself why I couldn't make progress in my recovery, even with small steps. It became clear that I needed to simplify things starting with the basics like sleep, nutrition and how well I was allowing my body to recover, both mentally and physically.

The concept of worthiness is interesting to me because I see it in people close to me who struggle to make changes despite having the time and resources. It's hard to tell if they really lack time, or if it's simply used as an excuse. After all, if people don't make time for their health and wellness, how will they make time to deal with illness?

For me, I need to invest in both areas taking care of my body through proper eating, sleeping, exercise, and adopting a holistic approach to mental health. It's about balancing all aspects of wellbeing, rather than waiting for the perfect moment or motivation to strike.

People often think stress is all about the fight-or-flight response. However, stress is far more complex, and we need to evolve our understanding of it in order to manage and mitigate its effects.

Coming out of the shadows to begin my advocacy work for first responders.

Interestingly, there are other, more adaptive stress responses. One of these is when the body releases oxytocin, which enhances our capacity to connect with others. This is when stress prompts us to seek help, a response that's often overlooked but incredibly powerful. This is known as the "courage response". As a first responder, I've experienced this firsthand. In moments of intense stress, rather than freezing or fleeing, I immediately act. It's a response wired into me, allowing me to face challenges head-on without hesitation. This kind of stress, where action is taken with courage and purpose, is something I've come to understand and rely on.

A few years ago, several friends lost their lives to suicide. I was upset and empathised with their families, but I was also very frustrated and angry that the pattern of inadequate mental health resources and awareness of the potential injuries for police officers was constantly ignored by organisations and government bureaucracy. I remember contacting a local radio station in Darwin on a talk-back segment on the lives lost to mental health within the police force. I was anxious but I needed to express the feelings of despair and devastation for the officers I worked with, and I wanted to see a change in the way mental health was handled in the police force.

At the time, if three teachers had committed suicide within a two-month period it would be all over national news. So, I sat in my car listening to the interviews on the radio. I felt nauseous, my stomach was spinning, and I was sweating but I pushed through and made the call. I went straight through and spoke with Katie Woolf on Mix FM. She was really nice and understood how difficult it was for me to speak. I was mindful that what we were discussing was raw and other people listening could have been affected.

So, I answered different questions and provided insight into the situation. All I hoped for was change. I finished the interview, and I was exhausted, mentally and physically. I went home and fell asleep for several hours.

While I was asleep my phone was pinging constantly. I remembered picking it up and saw I had so many messages and missed phone calls. I went outside somewhere quiet and began listening to the voice messages and reading the text messages. I couldn't comprehend how much gratitude there was for what I had said on the radio; it changed something inside of me. The feeling of loneliness was no more, I felt worthy and supported again ... a feeling that was missing for almost seven years. I started to believe in a new purpose and direction for my life.

Several days later, I received a text message from an ABC reporter who enquired about another interview. I then attended an interview with Jo Laverty from the ABC Darwin breakfast show, as she was investigating the current climate of mental health in the NT. The conversation with Jo was comforting, and I appreciated that the issue was taken seriously. I was happy with how the interview went and several days later I was contacted by another ABC journalist who wanted a more in-depth interview so it could be published on the ABC website.

I felt the pendulum of my life begin to swing the other way. At this point, I was living back in Melbourne, so I interviewed over the phone. It went on for an hour, and I was asked if I could go to ABC Melbourne to meet up with a photographer for the article. I met up with a great crime scene photographer who was so nice and clearly understood my passion for mental health. We even discussed her mental health which I enjoyed very much. I started to believe that people felt comfortable being open with me and confided in me; it was a quality I didn't realise I had. She took many photos and made me feel like a movie star (without the money!), and the article was published online and is still there today.[6]

I gathered momentum with a newfound direction. I began writing emails to various mental health organisations, Beyond Blue, Phoenix Australia, Black Dog Institute, Lifeline and so many more, just to enquire how I can help others on this journey. Finding this new direction was a weight off my shoulders. I realised the path I was on had changed but ultimately, I was still doing what I loved: engaging and helping people. I joined the Beyond Blue Ambassador speakers program. It was a great avenue to inform the community about the resources and support Beyond Blue could assist with.

The hardest part of joining was being open to telling my story to others without triggering any negative thoughts within the audience. I prepared my story over several days and it was approved. The first time I spoke was nerve-racking. I had to be mindful of what was happening internally, not thinking about what people would think of me, what I said, or whether they fully comprehended my story. When the questions began from the audience, I felt a sense of relief. I felt worthy and wanted again.

I enjoyed public speaking, especially because I felt so comfortable with the topic. While I had a commitment to Beyond Blue, I was involved in other speaking events at Parliament House in Melbourne sharing my story with 200 Victorian police officers. It was a daunting situation to speak in front of so many people. I remember the day so clearly, travelling into the city, being ushered through

---

6 - Roussos E. "Former NT Police officer calls for an overhaul of mental health services following recent suicides", *ABC News*, 2022 May 12. https://www.abc.net.au/news/2022-05-12/northern-territory-police-mental-health-suicide/101038706

by security into the main hall. I brought a USB stick with some slides to help me through the presentation. Then I hit a problem. I couldn't use my presentation; I began to get anxious and hot, feeling my face was on fire. The organiser told me I didn't have to do the presentation but I thought, *I'm here now with nothing to lose but my dignity of failing to share my story.*

I went up on the stage, nervous but committed to proving to myself I had the ability to overcome another obstacle. I started talking. It was strange but I could tell I was speaking fast so I took a big breath, letting it flow out of my chest and started speaking again. I was now comfortable sharing my story for over an hour, watching the faces in the audience all staring at me. I thought initially that I was saying the wrong things or people didn't understand what I was saying, as all I saw were faces looking directly back at me.

I finished talking and was then surprised by the applause. I asked if anyone had questions, and another 30 minutes went by as I answered everything that was asked. I walked off stage greeted by handshakes and pats on the back. It was such a rewarding experience. Driving home I was able to reflect on the event. I was exhausted, but I felt amazing. I began making posts on LinkedIn about looking after my mental health. The connections I was making increased a hundred-fold.

> People with a purpose in life are less likely to experience conflict when making health-related decisions and are more likely to self-regulate when making these decisions and consequently experience better (mental) health outcomes (Kang et al., 2019).[7]

---

7 - Schippers MC & Ziegler N. "Life Crafting as a Way to Find Purpose and Meaning in Life" *Front Psychol.* 2019 Dec 13;10:2778. doi: 10.3389/fpsyg.2019.02778

Heart2Heart Walk media conference at the
National Police Memorial. (Canberra, ACT)

I joined the Heart2Heart project and created a foundation and a national walk for first responders' mental health and premature mortality. It enabled me to connect with people on all levels of government and make some lifelong friends. I went from organising kids' birthday parties to a primary role in the official launch at Parliament House in Canberra. The almost 3,000-kilometre walk commenced on 1 July 2023 from Lambert Centre of Australia, near Finke NT (Heart of Country), to Australian Parliament House (Heart of Nation) via the National Emergency Services and National Police Memorials on 28 September 2023, a day prior to National Police Remembrance Day. I walked through 39 townships with a total population of just over 433,000 people. The objectives of the walk were as follows:

1. Raise awareness of mental health and wellbeing for serving and retired (veteran) first responders and their families.

2. Seek commitment from the Federal Government to implement all of the 14 recommendations from the 2019 Australian Senate Inquiry: "The people behind 000: mental health of our first responders", and specifically into First Responder Suicide, Post Traumatic Stress Disorder (PTSD) and Premature Mortality.

3. Raise funds in order to:

    a) Undertake academic research to obtain empirical evidence into the impacts upon serving and retired first responders' mental health and wellbeing to devise strategies to deal with the same.

    b) Explore and provide meaningful and positive education opportunities for first responders, past and present, and their families, to better support them all.

4. Establish a National First Responder Mental Health and Wellbeing Commission to provide greater command, communication,

coordination, and leadership of effort, to complement the Defence and Veteran's Suicide Commission.

Australian Government Response to Senate Inquiry Report Recommendations

On 27 March 2018, the Senate referred "The role of Commonwealth, state and territory governments in addressing the high rates of mental health conditions experienced by first responders, emergency service workers and volunteers" (herein collectively referred to as "first responders") to the Senate Education and Employment References Committee (the Committee) for inquiry.

On 14 February 2019, the Committee delivered its final report, which made 14 recommendations that seek to address the high rates of mental health conditions experienced by first responders.

Of the 14 recommendations, the (then) Australian (Coalition) Government:
- "supported in principle" eight (8) recommendations
- "noted" five (5) recommendations
- "supported" only one (1) recommendation.

Recommendation 1: The committee recommends that the government work with state and territory governments to collect comprehensive data on the occurrence of mental health injuries and suicide in first responders.

Government Response: **Support in principle**

Recommendation 2: The committee recommends that the federal government work with state and territory governments to collect data on the cause of death for first responders who die while employed or die within 10 years of leaving their service.

Government Response: **Support in principle**

Recommendation 3: The committee recommends that federal, state and territory governments work together to increase oversight of privately owned first responder organisations.

Government Response: **Noted**

Recommendation 4: The committee recommends that a Commonwealth-led process involving federal, state and territory governments be initiated to design and implement a national action plan on first responder mental health.

Government Response: **Support (still waiting in September 2024)**

Recommendation 5: The committee recommends that compulsory first responder mental health awareness training, including safety plans, be implemented in every first responder organisation across Australia.

Government Response: **Support in principle**

Recommendation 6: The committee recommends that compulsory management training focusing on mental health, such as that developed by the Black Dog Institute, be introduced in every first responder organisation across Australia.

Government Response: **Support in principle**

Recommendation 7: The committee recommends that mental health support services be extended to all first responder volunteers.

Government Response: **Support in principle**

Recommendation 8: The committee recommends that the Commonwealth Government establish a national stakeholder working group, reporting to the COAG Council of Attorneys-General, to assess the benefits of a coordinated, national approach to presumptive legislation covering PTSD and other psychological injuries in first responder and emergency services agencies. This initiative must take into consideration and work alongside legislation already introduced or being developed in state jurisdictions, thereby harmonising the relevant compensation laws across all Australian jurisdictions.

Government Response: **Support in principle**

Recommendation 9: The committee recommends that the Commonwealth Government, in collaboration with the states and territories, initiate a review into the use of independent medical examiners (IME) in workers' compensation.

Government Response: **Noted**

Recommendation 10: The committee recommends that the Commonwealth Government establish a national register of health professionals who specialise in first responder mental health.

Government Response: **Noted**

Recommendation 11: The committee recommends that a consistent approach to referrals to rehabilitation counsellors be developed across states and territories, requiring referrals to be made by general practitioners not associated with employers or insurers.

Government Response: **Noted**

Recommendation 12: The committee recommends that early intervention mental health support services be made available to all employees of first responder organisations with the aim of preventing or reducing the severity of mental health conditions.

Government Response: **Support in principle**

Recommendation 13: The committee recommends that the Commonwealth government make funding available for research in the prevalence of mental health conditions in retired first responders.

Government Response: **Noted**

Recommendation 14: The committee recommends that ongoing and adequate mental health support services be extended to all first responders who are no longer employees of first responder organisations around the country.

Government Response: **Support in principle**

I orchestrated that the main launch would coincide with Valentine's Day (14 February), exactly four years after the enquiry which, to be honest, has been disappointing for the first responders and emergency services of Australia with governments forgetting the selfless work we all did without seeking reward or gratitude only supporting one recommendation that was not even completed.

Over many months liaising with government officials and key stakeholders in the mental health sector we achieved a successful launch with keynote speakers, traditional first Nations Custodian Aunty Violet, former Commander Grant Edwards APM, CEO of Phoenix Australia Nicole Sadler, AM CSC, Allan Sparkes CV OAM, VA, FRSN, the Attorney General of Australia the Honourable Mark Dreyfus, Senator Anne Urquhart, Senator Jackie Lambie and Senator David Pocock. I had the privilege of speaking in the mural hall with such important people from the Australian government. It was an experience I will never forget. I've reflected many times since that event about the windy road I travelled from the despair of a mental health injury to rubbing shoulders with the policy makers of this great country.

The walk was successfully completed with only a few hiccups, but everyone arrived home safely and very tired. Former police officer Matt O'Brien, a great friend, started the Heart2Heart podcast with many interviews and visually recorded the walk with epic footage and insight into the walk. So many wonderful people were involved in the walk, I couldn't thank them enough for their commitment which not only raised awareness of the issue but also positively affected their individual mental health along the journey with a show of incredible resilience and strength to complete the job.

After the walk, my profile continued to grow in the sector. I began a role with Lived Experience Australia as a Board Director which has been incredible. I then joined

Mind Blank who have truly amazing programs educating the community about mental health awareness. I soon became one of the top 10 voices in mental health in the country on LinkedIn which was a terrific accolade.

I sometimes pinch myself looking back now that I've covered so much distance from when I was first diagnosed. It's important for people to understand that it's not a life sentence to have a mental health injury. You can change your direction with hard work, resilience and a never-give-up attitude. Feeling that I can contribute again to the community from a different angle is life-changing.s

The only downfall of being in the public domain is being critically aware people always want answers to their own problems. I have and will always listen to anyone who needs an ear but I'm very careful to disclaim I'm not a mental health professional. I've had to turn off social media at some points over the past few years due to people contacting me when they're suicidal and wanting to end their life. It's a lot to take on, being mindful that one wrong word could push someone in a devastating direction. So, I've been focused on listening and trying to guide people in the right direction without offering too much specific advice.

Continued curiosity is especially important while I continue to refine my purpose and look at what possible career paths I could use my skills in whilst maintaining my values with a growth mindset.

> Recent research suggests that health benefits of having stronger purpose in life are attributable to focused attention to and engagement in healthier behaviours (Kang et al., 2019). Indeed, stronger purpose in life is

associated with greater likelihood of using preventative health services and better health outcomes (Kim et al., 2014).[8]

The value of lived experience can't be underestimated. It speaks volumes and gives other people who are similarly circumstanced credibility that what I've encountered in my journey will hopefully create enough change to prevent and minimise mental health in the community. First responders are highly trained individuals who are the first to arrive and provide assistance at the scene of an emergency.

The term "first responder" can also apply to volunteers and emergency control centre workers who perform these vital functions in critical, time-sensitive scenarios. Australia is home to over 80,000 full-time emergency workers who play a crucial role in the community. Their work often involves dealing with serious injuries, potential fatalities, and imminent threats to life, safety and property.

The nature of their jobs exposes them to highly challenging environments and repeated traumatic experiences, both directly and indirectly. They often work irregular shifts, endure long hours, and face the constant pressure of making critical decisions in time-sensitive situations. Despite these demands, they continue to perform these vital duties day in and day out, year after year.

The mental health of first responders is increasingly becoming a focus of attention in Australia and around the world. It is now widely recognised that first responders are at a heightened risk of developing significant, ongoing stress, which, if not addressed, can lead to mental health conditions such as anxiety, depression, or post-traumatic stress disorder (PTSD). This growing awareness highlights

---

8 - ibid.

the need for better support systems and interventions to protect the mental well-being of these essential workers.

> Whilst in some situations, such as issues of social disorder, floods and cyclones, it is possible to predict and prepare for the likelihood of an event, it is rarely possible to predict the degree of severity or damage, and in many cases incidents (such as road accidents, house fires and homicides) arise randomly and unpredictably.[9]

The challenges are considerable:

> These include how to staff first responder organisations to accommodate some recovery time from the inevitable stresses of their role; how to prepare first responders for the psychological risks of the job without undermining the motivation and spirit that attracted them to the work in the first place; how best to provide in-service psychological counselling and training to maximise personal resilience while also enhancing the ability of the organisation to identify in good time people in need of help; how to honour the courage of those who do seek help in an organisational culture that also honours resilience and capacity to keep on responding in times of danger and crisis.[10]

The University of Adelaide Centre for Traumatic Stress Studies reports that emergency service workers face occupational hazards which present a risk to their mental

---

9 - Kanakis K & McShane C. "Preparing for disaster: preparedness in a flood and cyclone prone community" *Australian Journal of Emergency Management.* 2016 April;31:2. https://knowledge.aidr.org.au/resources/ajem-apr-2016-preparing-for-disaster-preparedness-in-a-flood-and-cyclone-prone-community/

10 - Senate Standing Committees on Education and Employment 2019, *The people behind 000: mental health of our first responders*, "Chapter 2: Why first responders?", SSCEE, Canberra.

health, describing the high rates of mental health disorders in this cohort as a "predictable phenomenon".

> In essence, it is the cumulative exposure to horrific accidents and lifethreatening events, as well as the personal threat to the individual officers, that leads to a cumulative risk of developing a range of mental health disorders. It is striking that there is little actuarial modelling of this risk of mental [health disorders] during the career of an emergency service worker in any of the emergency services.[11]

It is unclear how many first responders experience barriers to care and stigma regarding mental health care, and how this influences their help-seeking. The Royal Australian and New Zealand College of Psychiatrists (RANZCP) concurred that most first responders are exposed to trauma repeatedly.

> Exposure to trauma or "critical incidents", such as disasters, interpersonal violence, traffic accidents, and combat, forms an important part of the work of first responders and emergency service personnel. Research on Australian firefighters provides a valuable snapshot of trauma exposure in emergency services. A study on South Australian metropolitan firefighters found that 76% of the workforce reported exposure to 10 or more critical incidents throughout their career, and almost all those involved reported witnessing death on the job.[12]

Dr Brian White, a consultant psychiatrist and member of the International Society for Traumatic Stress Studies, describes mental health conditions as being "broadly proportional"

---

11 - ibid.

12 - ibid.

to exposure to trauma, outlining several factors that can determine how individuals respond over time to these experiences. While training, support and general health are important and play a role, Dr White states that exposure to traumatic experiences is the key factor.

> The most significant factor is the number and severity of these traumatic experiences. The second most significant factor is the management of people after they have had such experiences. Poor support and isolation if not outright aggression and intimidation will significantly aggravate these conditions. There are several other factors which are important; including effective training, effective leadership, physical fitness, having a clear mission and positive community support are all important. However, in terms of the relative contribution to the production and perpetuation of psychiatric syndromes are less significant than the actual traumatic experiences.[13]

Thirty-nine per cent of emergency responders are diagnosed with a mental health condition at some point in their life. They are diagnosed with PTSD at a rate two times higher than the general population.

I know firsthand the importance of having conversations and being open to assistance when visualising an ideal life, identifying passions, and creating a roadmap to get there. Many organisations are available to help with life coaching and career transition; I have used multiple avenues to enable me to take a step back using deep reflection and find my why and my purpose. At one point I engaged a psychotherapist who helped me identify what meaning and purpose was important in my life. After several meetings,

---

13 - Dr Brian White, *Submission 13*, p.1.

I gained a better understanding of who I was, and I discovered strengths I possessed that pointed me in the right direction. Through this exploration of the possible paths to take, understanding my values and goals in life has been substantial in how I see worth in this world.

The simplest thing I can suggest is to write down what values and goals are important to you. Just seeing them in a visual context allowed me to more clearly explore areas where my life aligned with those values, which in turn helped me feel more fulfilled.

Exploring my unique identity and improving my awareness has allowed me to feel more connected to my identity. It wasn't all smooth sailing as fears of being unworthy crept in. I've always attempted to heal past wounds by making sense of what's happening in my life right now, being present, learning from what happened in my past and moving forward with courage whilst integrating new healthier ways of managing my life.

Some things that have helped me find new purpose in my life which reduced some of the anxiety symptoms.

1. Keeping a journal of the situations that make me feel anxious and identifying how my body reacts in each situation. This can help me find what potential triggers increase my anxiety.

2. Maintaining and looking after my physical health. Regular exercise helps me target stress that I may be feeling, allowing tension to subside while my brain releases endorphins improving my mood.

3. Opening up to people who I trust and having discussions about any subject gives me relief and a better understanding of my worries and stressors.

4. Learning breathing techniques, relaxation exercises, and mindfulness helps me calm my mind.

Ultimately, the only person who helped me continue to explore my purpose and direction was me. I'm responsible for putting thoughts in my head and I'm responsible for removing them. Everyone has the ability to make their own decisions, even if it feels out of reach.

I know I possess resilience inside of me, proven by the fact that you are reading this book! It's always been there, I just forgot how to tap into it. When I did it allowed a continued push forward to never stop learning or trying different things, even if they feel uncomfortable. I simply allow myself to sit in the uncomfortableness and become stronger with more capacity to be uncomfortable without damaging my mental health. I'm more deliberate with the decisions I make which brings more satisfaction resulting in a greater connection with my purpose and wellbeing.

Always remember expectations versus reality. What my expectations are may be totally different to yours. I don't fully know what my direction or pathway is right now, but I'm enjoying the journey of discovering more about myself and what's exciting is that the possibilities are endless! Just one step at a time, mindful to always love myself in what I've achieved so far.

5

Mind Awakening

A man wearing an orange robe approached me.

After many years of trying various medications, some with side effects that totally drained me to the point where I was a shadow of myself. I was so tired, so over the never-ending med changes and having the same discussions with psychiatrists, psychologists and other medical professionals … I was at a crossroads.

I needed to try something different, a new direction. All I wanted was to get back to a normal life and stop thinking that I was so unworthy and feeling guilty and worried about my future. I enlisted the help of Dr Google, and began to research different treatments, theories and resources for a holistic approach to recovery.

Medication only masked the issues and never dealt with the problems. So, wakening your mind is a journey, it has many paths, twists and turns the most important part is that I continue to move forward, forgetting to dwell on the past, yes, I've made many mistakes throughout my life but that's how we learn, understanding what's important, knowing when to say no and improve the quality of my life.

"Hello," said the man in the orange robe as he gracefully approached me. I truly believe this meeting was a life-changing turning point, something which for a long time I had been hoping for. I sat outside in the courtyard. He didn't appear to be anything significant in stature, but he had a wonderful smile and presence. It was strange to have the constant noise in my head suddenly die down as I focused on his every word.

He said, "What do you truly feel is holding you back from being at peace with your past?"

I was taken aback by his eloquent question. I sat there with a blank look on my face, my body started to get hot and shaky and then my eyes started to well up. Small tears trickled down my face.

I felt shame and embarrassment that I was crying in front of a stranger. He just sat there pleasantly with a soft smile telling me that it's ok to feel the pain and to show my mind and body compassion. Happiness is not a state but how you relate to the different states you're in. The feeling of silence in my mind was a blessing, and I managed to control my thoughts as he began teaching me about Buddhism and why it was so enlightening.

I thought nothing could assist me in changing the way I looked at myself ... This negative energy consumed my mind for so long, but upon learning the art of reflection, I was able to see my thoughts weren't helping my recovery. From that moment my path was clearer, and I wanted to educate myself on how to improve my mental health. The monk asked what I knew about Buddhism. I didn't know much, only that I thought it was a lot about chanting, it was a very old religion and peaceful.

Buddhism is one of the world's major religions. It originated in India around the 5th century with Siddhartha Gautama (known as Buddha) and over the next millennia it spread across Asia and the rest of the world. Buddhists believe that human life is a cycle of suffering and rebirth, but that if one achieves a state of enlightenment (*nirvana*), it is possible to escape this cycle forever.

Buddha taught about the Four Noble Truths. The first truth is called "suffering" (*dukkha*) which teaches that everyone in life is suffering in some way. The second truth is the "origin of suffering" (*samudāya*). This states that all suffering comes from desire (*tanhā*). The third truth is "cessation of suffering" (*nirodha*) and it says that it is possible to stop suffering and achieve enlightenment. The fourth truth, "path to the cessation of suffering" (*magga*), is about the Middle Way, which is the steps to achieve enlightenment.

Siddhartha Gautama was the first person to reach this state of enlightenment. Buddhists do not believe in any kind of deity or God, although there are supernatural figures who can help or hinder people on the path towards enlightenment.

I was given a book. The first chapter was about Siddhartha Gautama, a prince who lived around the fifth century who, upon seeing people poor and dying, realised that human life is suffering. He renounced his wealth and spent time as a poor beggar, meditating and travelling but ultimately, remaining unsatisfied, settling on something called "the Middle Way". This idea meant that neither extreme asceticism nor extreme wealth was the path to enlightenment, but rather, a way of life between the two extremes was. Eventually, in a state of deep meditation, he achieved enlightenment underneath the Bodhi tree (the tree of awakening).

Buddhists believe in a wheel of rebirth into different bodies. This is connected to "karma" which refers to how a person's good or bad actions in the past or their past lives can impact them in the future. He was fully immersed in this religion and wanted nothing in return.

Physical fitness and mental fitness are entwined together.

Special people can turn up in one's life and inspire one to better yourself and to heal. Mastering my mental awareness was a foreign concept. Regardless of whether we succumb to a mental health injury, we should all make our mental health our number one priority. Without it, our body deteriorates and becomes overwhelmed with the lack of understanding.

In the early years of my journey, there was a rapid increase in knowledge as I tried to work out my recovery. I remember sitting in a conference room at the Austin Hospital with ten other emergency service workers. We didn't know each other but we were connected through the trauma we were all carrying.

One Wednesday afternoon, our instructor said, "Let's do mindfulness practice." I never heard of mindfulness. I sat in a circle with my colleagues, placed my hands in my lap, closed my eyes and listened to her voice. Some anxiety crept in because the hypervigilance activated and I didn't want people looking at me with my eyes closed. I was informed that I was going to do "Leaves on a Stream". She spoke softly and calmly as I tried to follow the instructions and to understand the different sensations flowing through my body.

Mindfulness

Mindfulness is also known as acceptance and commitment therapy (ACT). It is a tool to practise cognitive diffusion, to let go of thoughts that one is over-attached to and/or over-thinking about. Practising ACT is like untangling a fishing line (thoughts) that was twisted and knotted up. The first step is to recognise that *I am* the *observer* of my thoughts. I'm the only one who can notice my thoughts, enter conscious awareness, sit in the forefront of my awareness, and then leave awareness.

The biggest roadblock was to free myself from unnecessary emotional suffering to be willing to look at my thoughts in a new way. After the first session, I didn't think anything worked. I thought it was a bit wishy-washy and for hippies, but every day I would take some time in the evenings to practise mindfulness.

After a few attempts, I learned more about how my mind was working. Rather than choose to become "caught up" in negative thinking to the point of losing perspective, I began to let go of my attachments to that negative thinking. Getting myself into a daily routine was really helpful. It kept my thoughts under control knowing what I had to do and when.

It doesn't take long to do mindfulness. Most people have very busy days but, for me, just finding 10 minutes can change how I process my thoughts throughout the day or night.

According to Daphne M. Davis and Jeffrey A. Hayes in their article "What are the benefits of mindfulness?":

> Researchers theorise that mindfulness meditation promotes metacognitive awareness, decreases rumination via disengagement from perseverative cognitive activities and enhances attentional capacities through gains in working memory. These cognitive gains, in turn, contribute to effective emotion-regulation strategies.[14]

Every day, I face obstacles and I feel disconnected with no purpose or direction. It's important to acknowledge this truth not only internally but share it with others. Sharing what you're feeling or concerns can take away the loneliness and normalise your experiences and empower you to act.

I've always found it hard to relax, always on the move and my initial thought of attempting mindfulness or meditation was the lack of available time. Practising non-judgement and cultivating self-compassion through mindfulness has enhanced my ability to identify, describe, and differentiate my emotions.

So, I had to reflect on how I spent my time when I was procrastinating, avoiding or refusing to acknowledge I needed to do something. I was wasting precious minutes scrolling through social media or finding other excuses to not look after my mental space.

---

14 - Davis DM, Hayes JA. "What are the benefits of mindfulness?" *Monitor on Psychology*. 2012 July 1;43(7). https://www.apa.org/monitor/2012/07-08/ce-corner

Something most people take for granted is time. You don't know how much you have throughout your life but it is critical to never waste a moment; change your mindset to conquer, achieve, experience and love without hesitation.

I've learned to enjoy every new experience that comes across my path and absorb the adventure. There are numerous resources available regarding mindfulness, Spotify is a great one and I use the app a lot, so find the one that resonates with you. If my mind is still racing before sleep, I try journaling to clear my thoughts and promote a peaceful mind.

Unfortunately, many men overlook the benefits of mindfulness meditation, which involves intentionally observing the present moment. Instead of embracing this practice, men would rather argue about their right to be unwell than take the time to understand the workings of their minds. However, research has shown that meditation has multiple health benefits, including increased knowledge, stronger immune systems, improved memory, increased energy and increased libido. Combining breathwork with meditation allows us to reap the rewards of becoming better partners, friends and lovers.

> Mindfulness has been shown to enhance self-insight, morality, intuition and fear modulation, all functions associated with the brain's middle prefrontal lobe area. Evidence also suggests that mindfulness meditation has numerous health benefits, including increased immune functioning (Davidson et al., 2003; see Grossman, Niemann, Schmidt, & Walach, 2004 for a review of physical health benefits), improvement to well-being (Carmody & Baer, 2008) and reduction in psychological distress (Coffey & Hartman, 2008; Ostafin et al., 2006).

In addition, mindfulness meditation practice appears to increase information processing speed (Moore & Malinowski, 2009), as well as decrease task effort and having thoughts that are unrelated to the task at hand (Lutz et al., 2009).[15]

So, I was now on a path to opening my mind to new possibilities, without judgement but allowing myself to try. I met many psychologists throughout my journey. Some I connected with and others I thought had no idea what my job description was. Understanding a person's vocation is an important criterion to have, especially when talking to a first responder.

EMDR

Eye Movement Desensitization and Reprocessing (EMDR) is a psychotherapy that enables people to heal from the symptoms of emotional distress that are the result of disturbing life experiences.

I was sceptical at the start. I sat in the consultation room, getting myself comfortable on the sofa. My psychologist held a pen and began moving it from side to side and I followed the pen through lateral eye movements. This process was to help shift traumatic painful events to an emotional level, moving the guilt and shame to a more positive one: I did my job to the best of my abilities. It was the feeling of empowerment from those experiences that I saw my worth.

EMDR doesn't always work straight away and there can be blockages due to your medication and what other stresses you have at the time.

---

15 - ibid.

Light Meditation

Imagine looking at a bright light with your eyes closed. You see the red glow of your eyelids. Remember what that looks like.

I sat there imagining that light above my head travelling down towards the top of my head (picturing rays of light coming down). I would then imagine the light entering the top of my head and travelling towards the centre of my body, continuing towards the ends of my feet. I picture my whole body now filled with this warm yellow light (but it can be any colour) the light would then travel back up through my body and down again. I continued thinking like this for several minutes. Something amazing happens when I'm fully transfixed by the light.

This may seem hard to comprehend but I imagine myself lifting off the ground with the light continuing above and visualising looking beneath my body, I would then return to where I was sitting. My thoughts turned to my feet trying to feel the ground with my toes visualising that my toes began wrapping themselves into tree roots joining my body with the earth, fully connecting and present in my surroundings then releasing my hold on the earth and opening my eyes. It took a lot of practice to get to that point of connection, but it was very rewarding.

Chakras

I next directed my focus towards Chakras learning about how they align with my body and affect it physically and mentally.

> Chakra (cakra in Sanskrit) means "wheel" and refers to energy points in your body. They are thought to be spinning disks of energy that should stay "open" and

aligned, as they correspond to bundles of nerves, major organs, and areas of our energetic body that affect our emotional and physical well-being.[16]

Each of these seven main chakras is placed on different parts of the human body (see diagram).

The root chakra (Red) can manifest as physical issues or emotionally through feeling insecure about finances or our basic needs and well-being. When it's in alignment and open, we will feel grounded and secure, both physically and emotionally.

Sacral Chakra (Orange). Emotionally, this chakra is connected to our feelings of self-worth, and even more specifically, our self-worth around pleasure, sexuality, and creativity.

Solar Plexus Chakra (Yellow). It's the chakra of our personal power. This means it's related to our self-esteem and self-confidence.

Heart Chakra (Green). It's the middle of the seven chakras, so it bridges the gap between our upper and lower chakras, and it also represents our ability to love and connect to others. When out of alignment, it can make us feel lonely, insecure, and isolated.

Throat Chakra (Blue) is connected to our ability to communicate verbally. When in alignment, you will speak and listen with compassion and feel confident when you speak because you know you are being true to yourself with your words.

---

16 - Healthline, 2023, "A Beginner's Guide to the 7 Chakras and Their Meanings", viewed Jan 2025, https://www.healthline.com/health/fitness-exercise/7-chakras

Third eye Chakra (Indigo). When open and in alignment, it's thought that people will follow their intuition and be able to see the big picture.

The Crown Chakra (White or Violet). When this chakra is open, it is thought to help keep all the other chakras open and to bring the person bliss and enlightenment.[17]

Breath Work / Ice Baths

Opening my mind, becoming more aware of what is essential to my happiness and continually pushing forward, I began researching the benefits of breathwork incorporated with taking an ice bath. Sounds crazy but I still find this exercise a rewarding experience. Several breathing techniques helped me feel calmer and more relaxed when I'm dealing with high levels of stress. All I need is a quiet space where I can pay attention to my breathing. I attended a breathwork class followed by an ice bath not so long ago. Breathwork is a mindful practice that involves intentional control of the breath.

It is a holistic approach to breathing that goes beyond the automatic, unconscious process of simply inhaling and exhaling. By engaging in specific breathing patterns, I can positively influence my mental, emotional, and physical well-being.

So, lying on the beach side by side with a large group of strangers was exhilarating not only because of the beautiful location but we were all there to learn about the process of being with another human being who was connected to you and your thoughts. After my breathing exercise, we jumped into an ice bath on the water's edge. Everyone encouraged

---

17 - ibid.

each other to last two minutes. We then jumped into the ocean to heat our bodies up once more. Many benefits have been embraced by athletes, fitness enthusiasts, and those seeking holistic wellness.

*Be open to trying new ways of looking after my mental and physical health.
(Mills Beach, Mornington Peninsula, VIC)*

"Leaves on a Stream" Exercise

1. Sit in a comfortable position and either close your eyes or rest them on a fixed spot in the room.
2. Visualise yourself sitting beside a gently flowing stream with leaves floating along the surface of the water. Pause for 10 seconds.

3. For the next few minutes, take each thought that enters your mind and place it on a leaf … let it float by. Do this with each thought – pleasurable, painful, or neutral. Even if you have joyous or enthusiastic thoughts, place them on a leaf and let them float by.
4. If your thoughts momentarily stop, continue to watch the stream. Sooner or later, your thoughts will start up again. Pause for 20 seconds.
5. Allow the stream to flow at its own pace. Don't try to speed it up and rush your thoughts along. You are not trying to rush the leaves along or get rid of your thoughts. You are allowing them to come and go at their own pace.
6. If your mind says, *This is dumb* or *I'm bored* or *I'm not doing this right*, then place those thoughts on leaves too, and let them pass. Pause for 20 seconds.
7. If a leaf gets stuck, allow it to hang around until it is ready to float by. If the thought comes up again, watch it float by another time. Pause for 20 seconds.
8. If a difficult or painful feeling arises, simply acknowledge it. Say to yourself, *I notice myself having a feeling of boredom/impatience/ frustration.* Place those thoughts on leaves and allow them to float along.
9. From time to time, your thoughts may hook you and distract you from being fully present in this exercise. This is normal. As soon as you realise that you have become sidetracked, gently bring your attention back to the visualisation exercise.

Light Meditation

First, get into a comfortable position, and put your hands on your lap or your belly. Take deep, slow breaths. Remember, we are only going to take a few minutes to relax, breathe and heal.

Keep in mind that there is nowhere else you need to be, and nothing else you need to do right now. Next, close your eyes and imagine a healing warm light that starts to fill the space above you, like warm rays of sunshine coming down.

Picture this light in your head and imagine it slowly moving down your neck into your shoulders, down your arms into your fingertips, in your chest and core, down into your hips and bottom, thighs, knees, calves, arches, and finally, to your toes. Open your eyes and you're done!

Pursed Lip Breathing

1. Relax your neck and shoulders.
2. Keep your mouth closed and inhale slowly through your nose for two counts.
3. Pucker or purse your lips as though you are going
   to whistle.
4. Exhale slowly by blowing air through your pursed lips for a count of four.

Diaphragmatic Breathing

Practise diaphragmatic breathing for 5 to 10 minutes three to four times daily.

When you begin, you may feel tired, but over time the technique should become easier and should feel more natural.

1. Lie on your back with your knees slightly bent and your head on a pillow.
2. You may place a pillow under your knees for support.
3. Place one hand on your upper chest and one hand below your rib cage, allowing you to feel the movement of your diaphragm.
4. Slowly inhale through your nose, feeling your stomach pressing into your hand.
5. Keep your other hand as still as possible.
6. Exhale using pursed lips as you tighten your abdominal muscles, keeping your upper hand completely still.

Breath Focus Technique

As you build up your breath focus practice, you can start with a 10-minute session. Gradually increase the duration until your sessions are at least 20 minutes.

1. Sit or lie down in a comfortable place.
2. Bring your awareness to your breaths without trying to change how you are breathing.
3. Alternate between normal and deep breaths a few times. Note any differences between normal breathing and deep breathing. Notice how your abdomen expands with deep inhalations.
4. Note how shallow breathing feels compared to deep breathing.
5. Practise your deep breathing for a few minutes.
6. Place one hand below your belly button, keeping your belly relaxed, and notice how it rises with each inhale and falls with each exhale.

7. Let out a loud sigh with each exhale.
8. Begin the practice of breath focus by combining this deep breathing with imagery and a focus word or phrase that will support relaxation.
9. You can imagine that the air you inhale brings waves of peace and calm throughout your body. Mentally say, *Inhaling peace and calm*.
10. Imagine that the air you exhale washes away tension and anxiety. You can say to yourself, *Exhaling tension and anxiety*.

# 6

Being a Man

Every morning, I stand in front of the mirror with my thoughts looking at the face staring back at me. My mind wanders off to another place thinking about the past and the future. But one thing always remains constant: I'm alive, I'm worthy and I'm here, present in my life and excited about my future, careful not to look too far into the distance. We all have good and bad days. It's ok to feel a bit lost from time to time, but the new version of me is different and more self-aware about my body and mind and what's important.

When I look at myself in the mirror, so many other versions of me have contributed to where I am today, encouraging and opening my mind to endless possibilities. Continuing to build strength in my foundations and self-growth in gathering knowledge to better myself every day, complacency is not an option.

I choose to see the world the way I want to create the world and experience all its wonders. After so many years of recovery milestones and setbacks, life is about pleasure and meaningful experiences that expand my mind. It's ok that not everyone will understand my journey or chosen path. Being vulnerable to change with the possibilities of sharing my journey is truly exhilarating. It's like a voice in my head that kicks me in the backside, *Always keep on moving forward don't stop.*

I'm not meant to live worrying about how others perceive me, I'm meant to live staying true to the values that guide me through life. I remember the conversations and interactions with the Buddhist monk, my life is to be lived not controlled by my feelings of the past or the views of those around me or the anxiety about the future.

I must understand that people can only understand me in the depths of lived experience they have met themselves. I've never searched for gratitude or praise, so it doesn't control the way I conduct my life. Waiting for positive feedback is amazing when it's not foreseen but is not always given. I am the architect of my own reality, so I design a life that resonates with my true self. As a man, father, friend and lover, I embrace my uniqueness and let it illuminate the world around me.

Many aspects constitute what a man is, how they should act, their strengths, characteristics, values and so on. I'm not afraid to show the world who I am as a person who always understands the importance of personal values that have been instilled in me throughout the last 50 years. Having two young sons, I must lead by example. They can utilise my knowledge, wisdom and experiences on what is truly important about considering oneself and the relationships they develop. When growing up as a young man, I clearly knew the difference between right and wrong.

The most important message I can tell my boys is, "Men do not ever hit a woman." It doesn't get much clearer than that. Always respect women, care for them, love them and allow them the room to grow. Respect should be shown even before it is received. I've always had the strong belief that I must look straight into the eyes of my sons and see the potential for them to protect and uplift women.

During my policing career, I've witnessed many forms of domestic violence by male and female offenders. Trying to understand why people do this to each other when comparing my values was difficult. It was worse when children were getting hurt in these incidents.

Many cultures have an awareness of how they should treat each other. I respect all cultures but not how women are treated by some of them. True strength is expressed through active involvement in educating and modelling young men the importance of respecting women.

To teach my two sons respect for women, I must demonstrate respect towards women myself in all my relationships, professionally and personally. In reflecting on my younger years, children observe everything. They may not understand it all but it is visually processed and stored.

Having a role model to look up to is important. I always wanted to model myself on the right type of man. My father was a wonderful man, I saw the good things in him and the things I never wanted to be. It took a lot of courage to develop myself into the person I am today. I want my sons to witness my respect for adults, women and their female friends.

Verbal or non-verbal communication is critical when I explain to not only my sons but my daughters as well why I act and speak with respect, ensuring there is no confusion.

So much research and articles on how you should talk with children. Have you ever just had a conversation and said nothing, just listened and observed? Making time to understand my children's feelings is just as important, especially with so many pressures on young children these days. I didn't have social media or instant messaging as a child. The art of in-person conversations is disappearing. Now, if I don't want to deal with conflict, just send a text message or don't reply. This, of course, doesn't solve anything. Talking with your children about their thoughts and feelings might help find solutions to problems.

No one likes being told what to do, especially kids, but providing options for them to make the decision themselves develops that ability and self-confidence and promotes responsibility.

As a man, I am open to vulnerability and strive to improve my relationships through communication, trust and love. For most of my younger life and during my policing career, boys and men should suppress their emotions or hide their vulnerabilities; it makes them weak.

I tell my children to always act as if they are being recorded in public. Parents should always reflect on their behaviour because I guarantee some little kid is standing watching, thinking that it's ok to behave in that manner.

It is common for parents to shout obscenities at children at sporting events, but getting caught up in the moment isn't an excuse. And it is common for children to fake an injury to stop playing because of the anxiety due to parents pushing them too hard. Some parents want to live through their children, not what is chosen by the children. I have to promote being vulnerable in my children. It's a sign of strength to show how experiences affect me. I create a safe space for my sons to express their feelings and cultivate empathy towards the women around them.

So, what is vulnerability as a man? It is feeling exposed because of the uncertainty on how one is judged by others. Most men want to project to the world that they are strong and don't show weakness by shutting down the feelings of being vulnerable.

Stay with those feelings that make your body react, stay uncomfortable. I continue to be more open about my feelings and most importantly keep leading into difficult conversations that are rewarding. I know I will continue to be brave. Never apologise for how passionately you love.

Additionally, I am mindful of the media my boys consume, including video games, YouTube content and TV shows as they can often promote violence against women. As a parent and father, I have an obligation to be a teacher, coach or guide from an early age. I can shape my boy's values and cultivate genuine respect for women.

I believe that using positive approaches to communication and understanding the different ways my children interpret me and how my partner and I communicate can help to strengthen my relationship with my children and my partner. Everyone can have disagreements during personal or professional relationships, I've learned how talking about boundaries and having open discussions is important to a successful relationship.

Toxic Masculinity

Toxic masculinity refers to the way society pressures men to act and behave in certain ways. At its core, it's about toughness, rejecting anything seen as feminine, and striving for power. While it shows up differently for everyone, these traits often combine to create the stereotypical "manly" image you see in action movies or characters like Red Forman in *That '70s Show*.

Toxic masculinity in greater detail:

- Toughness – Men are strong, aggressive, and emotionally hardened.

- Anti-femininity – Men reject any and all feminine traits, including most emotions, accepting help and domesticity.
- Power – Men are worthy only if they have money, power, status and influence.[18]

Positive Masculinity

Positive masculinity is all about pushing back against shame, which often plays a big role in how many men experience emotions. Instead of focusing on limitations, it's about encouraging growth and highlighting what's healthy and possible in men's lives. It's about supporting men to build confidence, embrace vulnerability, and create stronger, more meaningful connections with themselves and others.

Many are resistant to change. The one thing in my professional life is constant in my personal life. The answer lies in showing respect to teaching respect. Every day I must respect my children, other adults and especially women. I encourage my children and adults that we should never use derogatory language when referring to girls or women and should never resort to violence or threats.

I've learned the art of actively listening to girls and women, respecting their opinions and not talking over them. I must ingrain the value of respect into my boys. Such discussions promote social awareness and conscience development in my boys and as they grow older, they should be taught about healthy relationships built on love and expressed through healthy and functional means.

These are conversations with both my girls and boys so they all understand when they should call out this sort of behaviour.

---

18 - Foss K. "What is Toxic Masculinity and How it Impacts Mental Health" *Anxiety & Depression Association of America*. 2022 Nov 14. https://adaa.org/learn-from-us/from-the-experts/blog-posts/consumer/what-toxic-masculinity-and-how-it-impacts-mental

By having these conversations, I foster empathy and encourage my boys to respond in more appropriate ways.

- Problem-solving and critical thinking: Teach them how to approach challenges logically and creatively.
- Financial literacy: Help them understand budgeting, saving, investing and responsible spending.
- Time management: Encourage planning, prioritising tasks and managing schedules effectively.
- Cooking and nutrition: Equip them with the ability to prepare healthy meals and understand the basics of nutrition.
- Self-care and hygiene: Foster routines for physical and mental wellbeing.
- Empathy and Compassion: Encourage them to understand and respect others' perspectives.
- Communication: Teach active listening, expressing themselves clearly and resolving conflicts constructively.
- Teamwork: The value of working well with others and contributing to a shared goal.
- Boundary setting: Help them understand and communicate their personal limits while respecting others' limits.
- Basic DIY and repairs: Skills like fixing a leaky tap, changing a tyre, or using basic tools.
- Technology literacy: Understanding and using technology responsibly, including cybersecurity awareness.
- Household management: Cleaning, organising and maintaining a living space.

- Emergency preparedness: Basic first aid, handling emergencies and staying calm under pressure.
- Emotional intelligence: Identifying and managing their emotions effectively.
- Resilience: Developing the ability to bounce back from setbacks.
- Curiosity and lifelong learning: Encouraging them to stay curious and open to learning new things.

I want them to understand more than just the physical aspects of relationships, the true feelings of connection on many layers enhance the strength of a relationship and they must grasp the importance of context and commitment.

Yes, my boys will eventually have girlfriends or boyfriends during their lives and I hope they will look to me for advice. I remember when I was younger having a girlfriend, I never stopped learning. I need to be able to let them understand when there is no genuine commitment in a relationship, they may mistakenly believe that no emotions are involved. Another continual value I want my children to understand is the importance of selflessness and gentleness, rather than entitlement and selfishness.

Furthermore, in a few years, I hope to teach them that touching, kissing, or being intimate with a woman requires her explicit consent. This important value is vital for not only boys but all men to embrace. Other men and I out there must redefine masculinity and help young boys create their own healthier version of it.

I'm just going to put this here; in case you're reading this and need a reminder the right person will know how to hold your hand, and the right person will love you and choose you just as deeply as you choose them. You will not have to ever feel like you love too much. You will not have to beg for the love you deserve; you will be someone's favourite person, and you will not be confused. You will not feel like you are fighting for someone who isn't fighting for you. One day you will understand. It never mattered how tightly you held onto the wrong people; people were always going to find people who were going to stay.

Being in a relationship and expressing love teaches my children the importance of showing honour and respect, even when it isn't reciprocated, while also understanding that true respect thrives with mutuality. I aim to model respectful communication in a loving relationship and guide my children to treat others with kindness, own their mistakes, and encourage positive behaviour. Respect begins with how I treat my children, interact with others, and especially how I show respect toward women. As a father, demonstrating the value of healthy relationships with women is a cornerstone of the lessons I want to impart.

I want my sons to feel comfortable expressing their emotions and discussing any topic without fear of judgement. By fostering strong connections with women, they will learn that vulnerability is not a weakness but a strength. It is essential to have open conversations with my sons about pornography and its portrayal of relationships between men and women.

These attitudes contribute to the larger problem of domestic violence and disrespect. Creating a safe and inclusive environment where young people can be their authentic selves is crucial. Like myself, my son has endured being bullied at school. It is disheartening to learn that many boys feel unsafe at school, fearing they won't meet the expectations of becoming a man, whether it's being cool, popular or tough. My greatest fear was a concern of becoming a target and I was targeted. Engaging in derogatory behaviour towards others was a misguided attempt to reinforce their masculine image.

There is a saying that always resonates in my head: kids are impressionable. I always wanted to be liked and looking back, I tried to fit in with everyone else. But I forgot an important part: me. Trying to fit in taught me the importance of staying true to yourself, a lesson I share with my children, reminding them that genuine connections come from being authentic, especially in a society where pressures can lead to serious mental and physical health challenges.

Being a man means embracing responsibility, integrity, and kindness while remaining true to yourself. It's about showing strength through vulnerability, respecting others, building meaningful connections, and striving to be a positive force in your family, community, and the world. True masculinity is not defined by societal stereotypes but by character, compassion, and the courage to live authentically and honourably.

When there is an issue that needs solving, I have previously fallen into the category that it is my duty to fix any problem. The key is to be more open and discuss the issue in detail. Solutions may present themselves and thinking outside the square by listening to another person's opinion can be helpful. If I'm talking about a sensitive topic, then I have to be mindful that I don't make it into a big conversation.

While I'm comfortable talking about most things, someone else can feel overwhelmed, making them too afraid to open up. Slowly encouraging conversations about sensitive topics needs to be flexible and I may not come to a solution straight away; re-visiting the topic later gives the other person time to process the information. Keeping conversations short may also be helpful.

I'm a proud man and I'm everything a man should be. I've found that one person who simply just takes my breath away, it's a feeling that I hope many people will find in their lifetime. It took me over 50 years and 8 billion people but there is one. Being a man doesn't mean rough edges. Being physically strong is very important to me but even more is being gentle and having an intimate side. The happiness in life amplifies when I'm in her presence, soothing her hair, adjusting her clothing when she can't see it and checking

I draw my energy from nature, the beach is my happy place.
(Mills Beach, Mornington Peninsula, VIC)

her makeup; these unconscious rituals reveal that she's acutely aware of my presence. When her focus shifts to self-grooming around me, it's an ancient biological trigger to enhance her attractiveness and gain my attention. These behaviours originate from humanity's evolutionary roots, stemming from a primal urge to appear groomed and fertile to a potential mate.

If you get anything about reading this book, don't ever stop being yourself.

Life is beautifully short. Live boldly, love with all your heart Smile every day and make the most of every day. Stop asking *Am I enough?* and start asking *Are they good enough for me?* You're more than enough, remember that. Relationships can be rewarding if you find the strength to open up and be vulnerable. I feel every bit of her pain through any of her struggles or obstacles, but I hold back and don't try to fix it for her. I know that in doing so, I would be depriving my partner of her own valuable lessons. But I will always be the first to put out my arms to raise her up after asking if she would like my assistance, rather than assuming she needs it.

I know she has incredible power and strength, and I respect that rather than fear it, or try to subdue it. I stand so firmly in my own divinity that I see her as my equal, and treat her as such, without undermining my unique gifts. I know that we need each other, that without one the other cannot exist. I stand firm in my purpose and my path knowing that all is as it is meant to be. I will continue to hold her beautiful soft hand through the darkness, the struggles, the laughter, and the judgements. In the face of adversity, I will continue to be brave and vulnerable to become a better version of myself.

A message for men, women and children:

> Don't underestimate the whole your absence would leave. ... Each of us, we're remarkable creatures and we have something to offer to the world, to the people we love ... It's our responsibility to make that manifest and we move a little farther away from Paradise every time that doesn't happen. Really, really. So ... this is serious business.[19]

---

19 - "Don't Underestimate The Hole Your Absence Would Leave", 2024 Aug 19, YouTube, Peterson J. https://www.youtube.com/watch?v=kEWD8m3hVbk

7

Feeling the Body

Have you ever just sat down by yourself and wondered why you feel this way? The most pivotal moments over the past ten years were developing my awareness of how my feelings reacted with my body, understanding the connection brought me more strength, resilience and courage to push myself further.

Major depression and anxiety were a roller coaster ride because my connection to my feelings was destroyed. Being a first responder, I became robotic in my duties and pushed all my feelings to the very bottom of my soul. After a time, the numbness settled in. When dealing with fatalities and serious assaults involving people, my mind was trained on not what to feel and to project an image of a strong leader until it was too much for my mind.

I've reflected many times over the years on what I could have done better for my own mental health. The knowledge of potential personal hazards and how to look after my health may have prevented my downfall and increased the time in my career. So, it is important for organisations to get this right and support the employees that support their organisations.

I know now that I never misplaced my feelings, they were still following through me. I just couldn't identify the connection of those feelings to my body. When I experienced strong emotions and was unable to identify them, those emotions interfered with my ability to lead a fulfilling life. My body was no longer in tune or the wiring from my brain was unable to establish my body's reactions to circumstances. I was more sensitive to emotions, tending to cry uncontrollably and the weight of self-pity held me down.

Many days were spent struggling with uncomfortable, overwhelming and unwanted emotions so re-establishing the connection with my body was critical. I had to start from scratch and learn them all over again, basically building a new and improved me. Learning new skills to give me the courage to expose myself to new experiences good and bad and giving my body time to sit uncomfortably with emotions has made me a stronger person.

There have been some instances when I've felt too much emotion and couldn't control my body's reaction. Like most families, growing children play sports outside or in stadiums. It was always loud and my senses were elevated on many occasions. It was not unlike the 2013 film *Man of Steel* when the young Superman begins to receive his powers. He can see and hear everything around him but can't filter the noise and function normally. When at a stadium, my hypervigilance was extreme. My heart rate was high due to all the people cheering and yelling.

I tried to camouflage what I was going through and appeared to cope with everything, but there were instances where my emotions shut my brain down for a short period, which was embarrassing and scary. On many occasions, I was asked to be a scorekeeper for the large electronic scoreboard. I would watch the game like everyone else, but I was unaware that I began to miss the children scoring due to the noise. Another scorekeeper would point it out but my reaction was that they were trying to cheat because my vision had never left the game. Then the same thing happened again the following game and I eventually asked my doctor what was going on.

He informed me that I was dissociating from my body. It was like a daydream, but I was wide awake. It was as if time had stopped but I was unaware. Then the fear crept in about the possibility of it occurring again. What if it happened while I was driving the car with my children? My doctor suggested noise-cancellation headphones to facilitate a more peaceful mind and the ability to control my feelings, so I did try it for a while. The children just thought that Dad was cool because he was listening to music with headphones on. I was very conscious about what people thought.

As my recovery progressed over the months, I left environments when it got too noisy but I still had to understand why my body reacted to those feelings.

Dissociation

> Dissociation is one way the mind copes with too much stress, such as during a traumatic event.
>
> There are also common, everyday experiences of dissociation that you may have. Examples of this are when you become so absorbed in a book or film that you lose awareness of your surroundings. Or when you drive a familiar route and arrive at your destination without any memory of how you got there.[20]

---

20 - Healthy Minds, "What is dissociation?", viewed Jan 2025, https://www.healthyminds.services/support/articles/dissociation

When I was in a difficult place, I couldn't just lock myself in a room. I needed to expose myself to discomfort so I could learn my reactions and how to cope.

I had headaches on and off and always assumed it was due to not drinking enough water. Placing myself in stressful situations and then feeling nausea or muscle pain at various points, I educated myself that it could be my emotions rather than a physical cause. My GP stated that it was my autonomic nervous system.

Autonomic Nervous System

> Our autonomic nervous system is a network of nerves throughout your body that control unconscious processes. These are things that happen without you thinking about them, such as breathing and your heart beating. Your autonomic nervous system is always active, even when you're asleep, and it's key to your continued survival.[21]

The autonomic nervous system produces your fight-or-flight response, which is designed to help you defend yourself or run away from danger. So, when I was under stress, this system kicked into action, and physical symptoms such as headaches, nausea, shortness of breath, shakiness or stomach pain.

I enrolled in an amazing research project with Phoenix Australia, and I participated in a course that enabled me to identify my emotions with my body's reactions to situations. It was called the Unified Protocol for Transdiagnostic Treatment of Emotional Disorders.

---

21 - Cleveland Clinic, "Autonomic Nervous System", viewed Jan 2025, https://my.clevelandclinic.org/health/body/23273-autonomic-nervous-system

Contemporary research highlights the shared features of emotional disorders, supporting a unified transdiagnostic treatment approach applicable to various conditions. The second edition of the *Unified Protocol for Transdiagnostic Treatment of Emotional Disorders* offers an expanded, eight-module therapy program emphasising emotion-focused techniques to address anxiety, depression, eating disorders, and more, with updated guidance for practitioners and streamlined, user-friendly patient materials.

To reconnect with my feelings, I learned about how I interpreted or reacted to my environment. I went for a walk in the rain and focused on the feeling of raindrops hitting my skin and enjoyed the warmth of the sun on my face. If I was experiencing frustration or anxiety, I grounded myself by taking my shoes off and walking on a grassy area just feeling the grass between my toes. Just understanding that moment to choose to feel an altogether different kind of relief.

As I've previously mentioned, it took many different treatments by trial and error. Being open to trying anything is the key to success. Some men are initially surprised at the idea of depression but then quickly feel validated and understood. Many men like me had the mindset that traditional masculine normality was to emphasise toughness, teamwork and competition and discouraged the expression of vulnerable emotions.

The inability to feel or describe emotions was hard but it's also considered normal among men. Having lived and educated myself about my feelings, I'm more aware of them and my empathy towards people has increased.

When dealing with the trauma of the past, I had to be brave and stop running away from my past pains.

I realised the importance of improving my ability to verbally express emotions, a skill women often excel at, by increasing my emotional awareness and identifying my feelings more clearly. Many men struggle with emotional intelligence and verbal expression, but by focusing on understanding my emotions, I've moved beyond logic to truly connect with how I feel.

> As a result of men's claimed low emotional intelligence, they are said to become strangers to their own emotional life, unconsciously transmuting their vulnerable emotions into anger and aggression, while also tending to extrude their caring emotions through the narrow channel of sexuality. …
>
> For example, one study of 1,285 men and women found that while women were more proficient at verbalising feelings, men and women were equally proficient at identifying feelings, and another study by Fischer et al. of more than 5,000 participants' ability to perceive facial emotions found "no gender differences in the perception of target emotions". Fischer et al.[22]

Emotional Intelligence

Increasing my emotional intelligence has increased my abilities to understand and manage my emotions in a positive way to communicate effectively, increased empathy to others and my resilience to overcome any challenge that comes my way.

---

22 - Wright P. "Men tend to regulate their emotions through actions rather than words" *The Centre for Male Psychology*. 2023 Aug 1. https://www.centreformalepsychology.com/male-psychology-magazine-listings/men-tend-to-regulate-their-emotions-through-actions-rather-than-words

Every day I know I'm building stronger relationships with every connection and achieving new personal goals. I know having a stronger connection to my feelings has enabled me to make informed decisions about what matters most to me.

Four key areas of emotional intelligence:

- Self-management – I'm more able to control impulsive feelings and behaviours, manage my emotions in healthy ways, take the initiative, follow through on my commitments and adapt to changing circumstances.

- Self-awareness – Recognising my own emotions and how they affect my thoughts and behaviour. Knowing my strengths and weaknesses improves and builds my self-confidence.

- Social awareness – I can understand the emotions, needs and concerns of other people after having developed new skills to identify emotional indicators. I am comfortable socially and recognise the power dynamics in a group or organisational setting.

- Relationship management – I now know how to develop and maintain good relationships and connections while communicating clearly, inspiring and influencing others, positively managing conflict and working well within a team.

By enhancing my emotional intelligence, I can better navigate workplace dynamics, inspire others and continuously expand my career opportunities.

The first step to improving emotional intelligence is to learn how to manage stress. Uncontrolled emotions and stress can impact my mental health, making me vulnerable to anxiety and depression. By understanding and controlling my emotions, I've learned to communicate openly and effectively, building stronger relationships. This has also helped me manage stress in the moment and adapt to increased demands. There was a saying in police work, "When the red mist sets in." It means when everything becomes cloudy, one can't make the best decisions.

I have used my emotions to make constructive decisions about my behaviour. When some people become overly stressed, they can lose control of their emotions and the ability to act thoughtfully and appropriately. Emotions are important pieces of information that tell me about myself, when faced with an uncomfortable situation or discussion it can take me out of my comfort zone and become overwhelmed.

I try to manage my stress and stay emotionally present, being able to make positive choices that allow me to control impulsive feelings and behaviour. It takes effort to manage my emotions in healthy ways, never sitting back and accepting them for what they are. I must take the initiative and continue increasing my knowledge about myself.

Through mindfulness and meditation, I'm able to connect to my emotions, the most important part being present and staying in the moment to understand the connection with my changing emotional experience. This is key to understanding how emotion influences my thoughts and actions. In both my professional and personal life, the utmost importance lies in the ability to establish connections not only with individuals but a strong connection with myself.

In the past few years, my understanding of the urgency of connection, both through verbal and non-verbal communication, has grown significantly. Recognising that connection plays a vital role in all relationships, I have come to appreciate its essential place in fostering a healthy partnership. Effective communication, encompassing both spoken words and physical touch, can greatly facilitate conflict resolution and the development of a more robust partnership.

Understanding how my body reacts to my feelings provides a healthy communication platform through which I can express my experiences, emotions and needs to others. By engaging in open and clear communication, not only can I meet my own needs, but I can also establish a sense of connection within my relationships. I firmly believe that clear communication is essential to avoid misunderstandings that may lead to hurt, resentment or confusion. Each relationship and individual has unique communication needs and styles, which require practice and effort to develop healthy communication patterns. It is important to recognise that communication will never always be perfect.

Being vulnerable, understanding my feelings and being open can be challenging, making it difficult for me to express my thoughts and opinions.

Some people may require time and encouragement to share their experiences, interests and concerns with their partner. Additionally, I love showing affection and appreciation, and sharing moments of intimacy which goes beyond solely creating a sexual connection. Intimacy is fostered through moments of closeness and attachment, where I can provide comfort, be comforted, and be open and honest. Intimacy can be as simple as holding my partner's hand or actively listening to her.

Connecting with others on both a physical and emotional level can have a positive impact on my overall health and wellbeing. Human connection encompasses the feeling of closeness and belongingness that arises from having supportive relationships with those around us. At this stage in my life, finding an amazing special person entering a new partnership, I offer my mind, heart and body as a gift to her. While the physical aspect of intimacy is undoubtedly important in any relationship, the quality of all encounters, moments and memories is deeply influenced by the level of connection established. We all understand the fundamental concept of connection, that primal and mystical feeling experienced in the presence of another person.

However, forming a deep connection with another individual is one of the most challenging aspects of a relationship, requiring vulnerability and trust. As an adult, it was easy for me to build walls around my heart due to the hardships, challenges and heartbreaks I had. To establish a solid connection, I must break down these walls only when I allow my partner to see my true self, both the good and the bad, I can build a connection that enhances all aspects of our relationship.

While intimacy can exist without an emotional connection, it is through this connection that I can experience a deeper and more spiritual connection. Always constantly studying my partner, learning a developing stronger feeling by opening my heart to her, I provide her with a pathway to a greater understanding of me. This, in turn, leads to a physical connection that is more fulfilling and exciting than we could have ever imagined. Love encompasses more than just physical attraction or enjoying the company of another person. It is about connecting with their souls and discovering the spark of light within them that teaches us more about ourselves and encourages personal growth.

Although creating a deep connection with her may not happen instantaneously, it is undoubtedly worth the wait. Sometimes love isn't planned, it's stumbling upon someone.

Never take things for granted and enjoy the raw, unexpected and beautifully unplanned connection. True love is a journey that starts with an instant connection and grows into something beyond words can capture. I embrace the unexpected because I know it can lead to a profound moment.

Become aware of emotions and how the body reacts, then you will truly understand how to feel.

8

Career Identity

Some days, I just reflect and analyse my thoughts. I also try to see my natural strengths and abilities. The biggest thing I feel down about due to mental health injury was the loss of my identity, my brand of the person I had worked so hard for many years developing. There was nothing more soul-destroying than knowing that my career was over and the uncertainty of not knowing how and when I could get back to contributing to society.

What I discovered through many years of recovery, my tool kit on how I looked after myself grew exponentially. I had a reputation for being a hard worker, honest, reliable, caring and so on, but how can I identify what the journey was to get back on my feet?

The initial years after being diagnosed with PTSD were a huge learning curve, trying to understand the information about what was needed for recovery, and how my mind was going to interpret the learnings and put them in place. There were many mornings staring into the bathroom mirror wondering where it all went wrong, then crying uncontrollably all alone with no one able to understand what was happening to me. I once had the responsibility of keeping lives safe and looking out for them but I had forgotten the most important person: me.

I no longer felt strong about who I was or what my identity was, and I believe it came down to three things: purpose, expectations and direction.

I knew when I joined the police force that I had a purpose: it was to look after the community, to save lives, and to investigate and apprehend people who harmed the community. It was very clear from the first day at the police fire and emergency services college that this was going to be exciting and rewarding. I couldn't wait to finish college and get out there. There is nothing more exhilarating than knowing what your purpose is. I had many expectations for my new career and how I would push myself to learn at every opportunity.

A-Watch Alice Springs Patrol group: what a team, what a crazy rewarding experience.

The first station I was assigned to was Alice Springs police station with 130 members back in 2003. The population of Alice Springs at the time was about 28,000, but that didn't include the surrounding indigenous communities. I remember arriving at the police station in the morning and we seven new probationary constables decided to go have a look at Todd Mall. We were stopped by another two police officers from the station. Instead of welcoming us, one of the constables just berated us for not wearing our hats. I thought to myself, *Oh, it's like this down here.* He was rude and I thought he was a bit of a wanker. So, we went back to the station to start our orientation, it went in one ear and straight out the other. I received my roster, and I was to come back for the night shift on the same day. That was something new to me, but I had no expectation of what hours I would be working.

My expectations of what my role was changed, and my initial expectations were no longer being met. The continuous workload on every shift increased so dramatically that during the early years working in Alice, I had to take a power nap during the night shift if there was the opportunity. I would drive to the top of Billy Goat Hill and sleep for 20 to 30 minutes. Those shifts didn't last too long, before I knew it, I would be attending over 30 jobs on a night shift and proactively patrolling the township. The money was great, lots of overtime but also a lot of paperwork.

My expectations of the judicial system diminished a lot through the years. I worked so hard with the people I enjoyed apprehending criminals to put them before a court just to have them released on bail by a magistrate. Back in 2009, I was on an evening shift attending a disturbance in Todd Mall when some indigenous people were intoxicated and fighting. A large male stood near Flynn's church being very agitated, yelling and pushing me around. I ran up to him and grabbed him by the left arm.

As I did this, he reached into the front of his jeans for his tomahawk. I just saw the tip of the blade and I reacted pretty quickly, sweeping his legs out, causing him to hit the ground hard with me right on top of him. I called the weapon, so my partner heard. I scuffled with the male (old-school policing). I managed to get control of the weapon, and then we arrested and handcuffed him. He was then placed before the courts the following morning. I thought it was great that there was one less person carrying a weapon I needed to worry about.

I returned to work that night, and I checked on the police information system (IJIS) to see how he went in court. I looked with disbelief, he was released on bail. *WTF?!* This was bullshit, it really was. Two days later, this same male was involved in a double murder. Go figure.

The workload increased and ultimately my mental health declined and I was ignorant of both my physical and mental state. I continued pushing on, but I had concerns about the direction I was headed professionally. Is this the career I want to continue doing for the next 25 years?

It took me years of reflection to realise that my unceremonious departure from the Northern Territory Police was exactly the way it should have been. I had finished my career there and my registered number was now obsolete. I had no direction in life except for falling into the abyss of trying to understand a mental health condition.

Since that day, I have had the privilege to speak with many first responders about how they were treated and the feeling of betrayal by our organisations that caused many of them agitation and is frequently the precipitating factor in their mental health decline.

In my experience, striving for excellence is key in any field whether it is emergency services, defence, corporate or construction. But the pressure to perform can often bring on Imposter Syndrome. This happens when people feel like frauds, even though their achievements clearly show otherwise. For leaders, who are constantly guiding teams and making big decisions, this feeling can be even stronger. The need to always appear confident and capable often makes it harder to deal with these doubts, turning the visibility that comes with leadership into something that feels more like a weakness than a strength.

To overcome Imposter Syndrome, it is essential for leaders to acknowledge its presence and understand that many others experience similar feelings. By normalising these experiences, leaders can create an environment where vulnerability is seen as a natural part of the human journey and not a weakness. Successful leadership requires creativity, innovation and a willingness to take risks. Embracing vulnerability opens channels of communication within teams, fostering transparency and connection. It is common for individuals to fixate on failures rather than celebrate their achievements.

As a leader, it is crucial to shift one's mindset and view failure as a necessary step towards growth and success. By celebrating both big and small successes, one can reinforce a positive self-image and internalise the concept of achievement.

Feeling isolated can magnify the effects of Imposter Syndrome. Regardless of the position or career stage, having a support network is crucial. Peers, mentors and coaches can offer constructive feedback and reassurance, providing an objective perspective that challenges self-doubt. Recognising the importance of having the right network and seeking assistance in achieving your goals is vital.

Additionally, pursuing professional development opportunities can equip leaders with strategies to enhance their confidence and overall leadership skills, effectively combating Imposter Syndrome. Overcoming it is an ongoing process that requires persistence and self-reflection. Challenging negative self-talk, acknowledging achievements and fostering supportive connections are essential steps in this journey. Leading by example and demonstrating vulnerability as a strength can inspire a more authentic, resilient and supportive organisational culture.

Imposter Syndrome can hinder personal and professional fulfilment. I experienced this when I faced setbacks and negative comments from others who doubted my ability to pursue a new career. However, I refused to let their opinions define me and used their scepticism as fuel to build a life and career that aligned with my passion for helping others. The lesson I learned is that people may project their journeys onto us, but it is crucial to stay true to ourselves and define our narratives.

To combat Imposter Syndrome, it is important to surround ourselves with people who truly see and honour us. When negative thoughts arise, our loved ones can guide us back onto our path.

Having a strong support system is vital, and it is important to express gratitude for those who support our dreams and help us recognise negative patterns. Comparing ourselves to others on social media can make self-focus seem impossible, but it is essential to remember that everyone is on a unique journey. Each person has a contribution to make, and by sharing our experiences and expertise, we can realise how much we have already achieved. Often, we become so focused on future outcomes that we forget to acknowledge our current accomplishments.

Sharing feelings of inadequacy with trusted individuals can reveal that many others also struggle with Imposter Syndrome. Saying these thoughts out loud can provide immediate relief. It is crucial to remember that we don't always need another degree, promotion or external validation to achieve something meaningful. Permitting ourselves to act is the antidote to anxiety. Along the way, we will achieve goals, learn new things and realise our potential to create a better future.

Some days, I reflect on my current position, the path I took to get here, and where I am headed. People often speak about the resilience needed to adapt to life's hardships and setbacks. While not every day is filled with positivity, it is crucial to ask ourselves whether we tend to bounce back or crumble when things go astray. Dwell too long on problems, and we risk feeling victimised, overwhelmed, or resorting to unhealthy coping mechanisms like substance abuse, eating disorders, or risky behaviours.

Over time, stress can take a toll on our psychological, emotional and physical wellbeing. Self-awareness involves understanding our thoughts, emotions and behaviours to better respond to stress and adversity and knowing when to seek support. Being open to change is a quality we often hear about, especially in discussions around purpose. Purpose statements have become powerful expressions of mission and vision, inspiring our personal journeys as well as those of organisations. Ultimately, they not only define an organisation's identity but also its aspirations.

Like the art of kintsugi, healing a broken heart requires patience, skill and care. It is a process of acknowledging our pain, embracing our emotions, and learning to let go of what once was. However, just as the mended piece in kintsugi becomes more beautiful than its original form, a heart that has been nurtured with love and care can also become more beautiful and resilient. The gold used in kintsugi does not erase the brokenness of the pottery; rather, it highlights the value of the brokenness itself.

Similarly, the cracks and scars of a broken heart do not diminish its worth or capacity for love. They serve as reminders of our humanity, our ability to endure pain and emerge stronger, and our capacity to love again, even more deeply and wholeheartedly.

We come to understand that our heartbreak has made us more compassionate and empathetic and that we possess abundant love to offer someone who deserves it. Our worth as individuals is not determined by our relationship status. Let no one make us feel otherwise.

Ultimately, staying true to ourselves and listening to our hearts is crucial. Settling for less than we deserve or compromising our values for the sake of a relationship is not the path to fulfilment. Love is meant to bring joy and satisfaction, and if it brings more pain than happiness, then it may be time to prioritise self-love.

Have the courage to overcome obstacles and love will find its way to us. For many professionals, first responders and executives, the pursuit of their careers consumes most of their time and energy. Finding the time and emotional space for love can be challenging, especially when it feels like there aren't enough hours in the day to accomplish everything.

One of the most important aspects of recovery is finding genuine connections and friendships with people who will support you and stand by your side during the darkest moments. They don't need to give advice; they just need to listen and understand what you're going through. Throughout my recovery, I've been fortunate to meet some truly amazing people. Among them are my close friends from my time in the Northern Territory Police, Will and Paula Dooley McDonnell. They are exceptional people, and to this day, they remain some of my closest friends.

I also competed in the Finke Desert Race for many years, just like their incredible son Jack, who is an outrageously skilled rider, having finished in the top 10 multiple times. The race, which began in 1976, started as a challenge for local motorbike riders to race from Alice Springs to the Finke Community (Apatula) and back. It is held annually on the Queen's (King's) Birthday long weekend, running along sections of the old Central Australia railway track, through red dirt, sand, spinifex and desert oaks. Although the railway was realigned in the early 1980s, the race continues on its original course.

Finke Desert Race 2012, Prologue Day … can't see I'm nervous at all.

The Finke Desert Race is often called the "Bathurst 1000" of motorcycle racing in Australia, and I've been privileged to compete in it seven times, with a 100% finish rate which I'm incredibly proud of. While I've never been at the front of the pack or in the top 20, just finishing this iconic race is an achievement in itself. Over the years, I've witnessed some great riders cross the finish line, including champions like David Walsh, Toby Price and Ben Grabham. Many other talented riders have won the race, including the late Daymond Stokie, an Alice Springs local who tragically passed away doing what he loved: racing motorbikes.

The Finke Desert Race is demanding both physically and mentally, and while it took a toll on my body, I cherished the experience. It became a personal challenge for me, but also a source of connection and friendship. I spent countless hours on the track, battling through physical and mental exhaustion. There were moments when I thought about how hard it was and whether I could keep going. But there was always another voice in my head telling me to push harder, to keep going, and that everything would be ok in the end. So, I did.

After each ride, I'd return to Alice Springs and catch up with Will and Paula for coffee. We'd have relaxing conversations about anything and everything, and that sense of belonging and being seen as a friend is something I'll never forget. They've always been there for me, and they still are to this day. I mention them in this book because I truly appreciate everything they've done for me and the people around them. They have a unique way of making people feel like part of their family, and they are truly special individuals.

The pursuit of professional success and the pursuit of love are not mutually exclusive. Investing in a loving relationship can bring balance to our lives, ultimately contributing to success in all areas. In the end, the key to building a strong and healthy relationship lies in self-discovery and personal growth. We must learn to love and accept ourselves, cultivating a sense of purpose and direction from within. Only then can we build a relationship based on mutual respect, understanding and support, capable of withstanding the test of time.

Approaching our partner or organisational leaders with empathy and understanding is crucial in building a relationship grounded in shared purpose and direction. By listening to each other's needs and concerns and expressing our thoughts and feelings with clarity and compassion, we create an environment of mutual respect and understanding. While it may be intimidating to open up and be vulnerable, it is a necessary step in building and maintaining a relationship.

Taking care of our mental and physical health is equally important. Engaging in physical activity boosts endorphins, while proper nutrition and sufficient sleep contribute to overall wellbeing. Being in the presence of a loved one increases dopamine and norepinephrine levels, leading to feelings of pleasure, excitement and euphoria. I had to embrace change, find my purpose, and mend my broken heart with care. Seeking knowledge is a key to recovery.

I began completing a skill matrix of what abilities and skills I thought I had to develop to rediscover my identity and change my path. It was difficult because I didn't have the knowledge and skills to complete such a task. So, I searched the internet for organisations that could assist. I found several and one organisation that still to this day stands next to me and provides guidance when I need it is Torode Solutions in Canberra. Their CEO, Sarah Torode, is someone who I call a good friend. With a wealth of knowledge that I have taken in my stride, it provided a great platform to expand my knowledge on how I saw myself in the world and the possibilities of what I could achieve.

In January 2022, I was asked if I was interested in joining a cause for first responder mental health, a 3,000-kilometre walk from central Australia to Canberra to raise awareness about suicide and moral injury. From March to May of the same year, I lost three friends to suicide. It really made me angry at how things had not changed since I left. I wasn't angry because of what they did, I was angry because organisations were still not listening to their staff and failing in their duty to provide a safe workplace for members and their families. I said to myself, *That's enough*, and I contacted media outlets in Darwin to advocate for first responders. This led me to radio interviews and newspaper articles, including with the ABC, and I found a new career speaking up for those who couldn't. A new identity was born.

9

Empathetic Leadership

The importance of identifying and understanding conversations in both personal and professional relationships is crucial to successful health and wellbeing. Throughout my career, I've had the opportunity to evolve under many leaders who have instilled some knowledge that I've been able to project onto others.

I have also come across some terrible leadership styles that relied on passive, passive-aggressive or aggressive communication. I have always been a believer that some people are destined to lead through their ability to connect on many different levels and their knowledge gained in listening to what is important and needed to move forward as a collective.

I have always wanted to be an honest and transparent leader; I have never been remotely interested in personal awards. It has always been about the team. Working together on an idea that has been discussed in collaboration can be empowering, not only for the leader but also for the people who come along on the journey. No one likes to be told what to do, but giving people a choice and the opportunity to be involved in decisions promotes reflection of self-confidence. Listening is different from simply being in a conversation. It means interpreting different voices.

Empathetic leadership means having the ability to understand the needs of others and being aware of their feelings and thoughts. Unfortunately, it has long been overlooked as a soft skill when it should be a strong skill.

In the ever-changing landscape of our careers, it is essential to establish connections and relationships that will enable us to succeed in any environment. I naturally look to our leaders for guidance and support. The true value of empathetic leadership is often overlooked and misunderstood compared to more authoritarian styles.

I have had the privilege of experiencing the generosity of an empathetic leader, it is important to acknowledge and promote these individuals. In high-stress environments, creating an atmosphere of understanding without judgement is crucial. Instead of seeking someone to blame, we should focus on acknowledging and validating emotions, using empathetic language to show support and acceptance. This fosters an environment of trust and collaboration.

Building connections and relationships are important professionally and personally; with the Chief Minister of the NT, Hon Lia Finocchiaro (right), at the Parliament House. (Darwin, NT)

Leadership is not just about authority; it is about empathy. It is about relating to and connecting with people, inspiring and empowering them to achieve greatness. Leaders have a responsibility for the wellbeing of those they lead. Without support and dedication, organisations cannot thrive. Leading by example and demonstrating qualities such as patience, empathy, sympathy and appreciation encourages people to stay and contribute to the success of the organisation.

So what is empathy? It is the skill of (1) connecting with others to identify and understand their thoughts, perspectives and emotions; and (2) demonstrating that understanding with intention, care and concern.

Empathy helps bond colleagues together and forms the foundation of a resilient and inclusive workplace. Although it is often underestimated as a business skill, empathy is essential to success in the future of work.

It is possible to cultivate and develop empathy. Empathy links to many positive outcomes that teams can leverage to become more agile and innovative in times of crisis.

There are three aspects of empathy: cognitive thinking, affective feeling and behavioural action.

Cognitive empathy, or engaging with employees to understand their thoughts, emotions, and perspectives; *affective empathy*, or sharing in or showing similarity to employees' emotional states; and *behavioural empathy*, or actions that communicate and demonstrate a sense of empathy for employees. Employee innovation refers to an individual's ability to generate new ideas, processes and approaches to achieving goals. Work engagement reflects employees' emotional investment in their work and the company's mission.

Today, the younger generations have become more aware of the importance of mental and physical health. They want to know that they will be taken care of. When support, respect and trust are evident, loyalty and commitment increase.

Looking back at the earlier stages of my work life, I did not have this mindset, it was all about making money to buy material possessions without any thought for my mental health. Being physically active all my life, only in the past 10 years have I truly come to understand the correlation between physical activity and mental health.

Empathy is the linchpin of effective leadership, and it can manifest in various ways across different communities. Understanding the importance of collaboration, morale and cultural competence, an empathetic leader actively listens and provides emotional support. They anticipate the needs of others through planning and offer practical solutions.

Both compassion and empathy are essential qualities, but they can also have negative consequences if not managed appropriately. Empathy enables us to connect with others and establish meaningful relationships that contribute to our overall wellbeing. It serves as a foundation for compassion, which, when put into action, brings about numerous additional advantages.

However, empathy is not without its challenges. It is susceptible to cognitive biases, meaning that we tend to empathise more with individuals who resemble us and project our own emotions onto those who differ from us. Studies have revealed that in regions throughout the world marked by intense conflict, individuals do possess empathy, but it is predominantly directed towards their own group while lacking empathy towards the opposing group. Simply absorbing the emotions of those surrounding us can hinder our ability to make sound judgements and result in unfavourable choices.

Additionally, empathy has the potential to result in emotional exhaustion. Constantly immersing oneself in the emotions of others can leave little space for one's own emotional wellbeing. It is vital to avoid becoming entrenched in feelings of sadness, anger or loneliness. When it comes to both empathy and compassion, it is essential to gain mastery over one's emotions rather than succumbing to them.

A key distinction between compassion and empathy lies in the requirement for action in compassion. Acting is an essential component of compassion, and it offers several advantages. Engaging in acts of giving back can contribute to a decrease in depression and anxiety, lower stress levels, and enhance confidence and self-esteem, among numerous other benefits.

One common challenge associated with excessive compassion is known as "compassion fatigue". This phenomenon is frequently observed in professions such as first responders, nursing and caregiving, and it manifests in physical symptoms such as anxiety, depression, difficulty focusing, aggression, and a sense of disconnection from reality. It is crucial to recognise and address these potential challenges to maintain a healthy balance in practising empathy and compassion.

Another important aspect of compassion is the possibility of being overly compassionate. While compassion is about doing what is best for someone, it is not always easy to discern what that entails. Sometimes, what may seem "nice" in the moment can enable negative behaviours, lead to unhealthy relationships, and hinder personal growth. In such cases, excessive compassion can inadvertently increase suffering instead of alleviating it.

In terms of leadership, both empathy and compassion play vital roles. Empathy helps to build rapport and trust within a team, fostering a strong foundation for collaboration. Compassion allows leaders to objectively manage the behaviours of their team members for the greater good, supporting them in overcoming personal obstacles and achieving success. Striking a balance between these two emotions enables leaders to create a positive and supportive work environment.

Ultimately, the distinction between empathy and compassion is less important than the ability to cultivate and develop both skills. By embracing empathy and compassion in a balanced manner, individuals can lead more fulfilling lives and positively impact those around them.

As organisations recruit individuals from different generations, it is crucial to appreciate their unique wants and needs. People from the 1960s to '80s value authenticity and leaders who acknowledge their individuality. On the other hand, those from the early '80s to the mid-2000s are more accustomed to digital communication and may demonstrate empathy through virtual support networks and inclusive practices. As leaders, we must continuously grow and adapt to these changes, learning from our experiences and evolving to better serve those we lead.

Scalability and empathy both play pivotal roles in achieving success. While hard work and individual performance are important, investing in education, training, and developing the right people matters even more.

In a collaborative setting, empathy is vital for creating an open and supportive culture that encourages honesty and facilitates improvement and growth. It is essential to recognise the unique strengths and challenges of each employee and offer flexibility in work arrangements to accommodate personal needs. Empowering individuals to achieve a healthy work-life balance showcases empathy in action. Transparency in communication is also crucial for building trust and reducing uncertainty.

Effective people management and recruiting the right individuals are key to success. Additionally, fostering empathy in collaborative work and promoting an open and supportive culture can create an environment where growth and improvement thrive.

As leaders, we should value and invest in our people, ensuring that their contributions are recognised. In many sectors, employees are capable, passionate and focused on their tasks. By consistently emphasising empowerment within organisations and encouraging self-reflection, we foster meaningful discussions for improvement. Positive recognition and rewards are crucial for acknowledging their hard work.

Developing empathy is important in any workplace, especially when stress levels are high. However, it is essential to understand that empathy alone is not always enough. When empathy is not used effectively, it can lead to challenges in avoiding conflicts, making decisions solely to spare other feelings, or failing to address underlying issues can result in more problems, burnout, and dissatisfying relationships.

Despite these challenges, fostering empathy is still crucial, particularly in tough times. Recognising and managing our own emotions is the first step toward building empathy. Letting ourselves become vulnerable to new supports and resources, and engaging in mindfulness and muscle relaxation practices can help acknowledge and manage our feelings, enabling us to empathise with others and navigate high-stress environments more effectively.

Building trust and rapport with our people as leaders relies heavily on validation and empathy. Acknowledging and validating their experiences, showing compassion, and understanding, and adjusting our approach to fit their needs are all important aspects of empathetic leadership. However, as empathetic leaders, we may face challenges in balancing others' needs with our own.

It is important to recognise and address these difficulties to achieve sustainable professional growth and personal fulfilment but also to be aware of our own mental and physical health. A greater investment in education and awareness of leadership is essential. Once there is an understanding, open discussions may take place without the fear of retribution but being honest and transparent will build trust and respect.

Effective leadership styles promote a safe place for employees through enhancing education on the sources and effects of domestic, organisational and operational stress; for example, normalising police service experiences and fostering a deeper understanding of the physiology and neuroscience behind the acute stress response. I would like to see some key skills developed or improved with first responders:

- self-regulation
- conflict management
- active listening techniques, such as paraphrasing, empathetic reflection, and the significance of advice-free listening
- cognitive-behavioural strategies
- strategic planning to enhance resources and practices for sustaining resilience and wellbeing

- creating an environment to allow open discussions with a focus on comprehending the mechanisms and impacts of both single incidents and cumulative operational stress on the body, brain, behaviour and relationships.

The additional training will gain an improved capacity to support peers. There will be an increased awareness of how personal first-response experiences affect oneself and colleagues, including the influence of gender on stress experiences and communication. Furthermore, exploring how to create a personalised psychological wellbeing toolkit and strategic plan to uphold resilience and wellbeing under operational demands will potentially mitigate overwhelming experiences.

10

For My Children

For many years, I've travelled many paths. Some led to nowhere or I got lost or trapped with no alternatives. I hit many obstacles but one thing that remained constant was having positive relationships with my children, my professional relationships and my intimate relationships. I understand the need for positive connections in both professional and personal relationships to reduce loneliness and enhance my emotional wellbeing.

Something etched in my memory was the day I became a father for the first time. It was one of my goals in life to experience happiness, learning, loving and protecting a child of mine.

I remember the birth of my first daughter, feeling helpless because I couldn't do anything besides support and comfort for my partner. The first night I walked the hallways of the hospital holding her in my arms sleeping peacefully, I must have walked for hours never wanting to put her down in case she woke up. It was a day I fell in love all over again and a new relationship started. This was a new frontier, with complexity and uncertainty, the uncomfortable feeling of ground that I had never travelled on before but I enjoyed the challenge of learning and trying to be a great dad.

I wanted to instil my values to help her reach her milestones, celebrate success and catch her when she falls.

Navigating the minefield of how I communicate with children effectively was both positive and negative. The learning curve was intense.

I always endeavoured to build and maintain good relationships with my children, encouraging those interactions to be warm, caring and meaningful as I focused on their needs and wants. Listening to them and providing a feeling of security is imperative to building trust.

When more children arrived, the relationships were all different as individuals. My children have various traits that make them so unique. The characteristics may vary but they all possess the same values as I do and understand the importance of caring, empathy and respect for each other.

Watching my children navigate their emotions through different experiences has been an incredible journey. Seeing how they interpret danger, feel safe, and interact with other kids while building their social skills has been amazing, though it's also made me more aware of how my own feelings are affected. The relationships I have with my children feel completely different from those with adults. There is no judgement, no discrimination, just pure acceptance. I love seeing them freely explore their surroundings, play and learn, knowing that I'm creating opportunities for their growth and helping them thrive.

I was amazed when the relationships with each child changed when they started school. Like sponges, they absorbed information quicker than I could. I think back to times when I asked a child if there was anything I could do for them, only to be completely surprised when they turned around and asked me the same question. The importance of social skills can't be underestimated. If you have children, think back to the time they first showed kindness and empathy towards you and how they felt when you were sad or happy.

There were good days and bad days, certain times of the day were challenging and emotional for my children as they had to separate from me when dropped off at childcare. I struggled with the crying and the desperation they showed in their eyes. As I continued my recovery so many thoughts spiralled out of control, I always thought I was hurting them at the drop-offs. I would pass the child into the carer's arms while they were in tears. I walked off in shame thinking my child would not love me anymore. The walk to the car felt like an eternity as I listened to the cries of my child.

It was something that really hit me in the heart. I would return home and contact the childcare to see if everything was ok; sure enough, everything was fine. I lost count of how many times that occurred.

While I was becoming more aware of my feelings as I improved, I had to be emotionally available to assist my children. It was difficult for me to show my feelings which complicated the relationship, but I became good at discussing feelings with them without me expressing mine.

Sometimes, just quietly sitting with them and listening to what they had to say was very important to me. Those moments with each of my children were special, not because of the activity. They grew up so quickly and soon enough I'll have relationships with my children as adults. I enjoy the moments when I'm in nature with all the children, the laughter and the conversations but most importantly enjoying that connection to me and the awareness they learn about the importance of disconnecting from social media being present in themselves.

Each day is never the same. While trying to manage finances, work and my personal commitments without showing them when I'm stressed, I have to help my children understand their own feelings and recognise these same feelings in their siblings and other people.

I know learning never stops and while I make mistakes, I strive not to repeat them, focusing on improving relationships without a set formula, just forward progress.

Expressing my love for my children through human touch is very important in every stage of their lives. I know my girls don't like me giving them a quick hug in public ("You're embarrassing me, Dad") but that's ok. I know when they really need one, they will receive one. I treat every interaction as an opportunity to connect with my children by giving them my complete focus; I make eye contact, smile and listen to everything they have to say.

Telling an adult that I love them is different to telling a child, I believe it's so much more important to tell them *every day*, no matter their age. When they're having a bad day or things aren't going as well as they wanted, I look for the opportunity to remind them that I love them unconditionally. A simple "I love you" after a phone conversation or a discussion can have a major impact on my long-term relationship with all my children.

The urgent connection starts with listening, not necessarily saying anything. I just have to acknowledge my child's feelings, I need to show them that I understand. I utilised some of the knowledge I acquired doing my master's in counselling, such as paraphrasing and active listening. By doing this, I reassure them that I'm there to help. Putting myself into their shoes and seeing things from my child's perspective empathises with their concerns which builds mutual respect. They understand they're not alone and we can achieve positive outcomes together.

I've always been heavily involved with my children's sports – swimming, football, soccer, netball, basketball the list goes on – so it's important that they all learn the necessary social skills to be respectful. I'm always watching and learning from them as they progress in their development of language skills.

I've learned that teenagers, much like adults, lead busy lives and still need attention and care. Taking the time to express emotions, fostering their creativity, and giving them my undivided attention is crucial. It doesn't always have to be about big sporting activities; sometimes, simple moments like playing a game of UNO or working on a puzzle together can mean just as much and help strengthen our connection.

One of the main obstacles I find with four children is getting one-on-one time with each child. It can be daunting some days when they are all trying to pull me in different directions, juggling my time and being adaptive to various changes. I try speaking without distractions.

Mobile phones are problematic. Just asking them to put the phone away is like saying there is no more chocolate in the world, or a potential Snapstreak will be over if I don't reply to Dad soon. I know they appreciate some quality time together. They must believe that my main priority is them despite the many distractions and stressors that come my way.

Encourage, encourage, encourage. I always encourage my children to make decisions. This builds their self-confidence. I'll be there to catch them when they fall but I want to build their sense of responsibility, accountability and personal achievement with no judgement, just knowing that they are loved, safe and secure.

11

Trustworthy and Dependable

Life is full of different relationships, every one of them is different. All relationships come with their own unique set of expectations, and the more expectations, beliefs or thoughts that arise, the more they can impact me internally. Understanding this helps me navigate the complexities of each relationship while staying mindful of my own emotional wellbeing. It's like a fine juggling act 24 hours a day, constantly trying to understand the dynamics that present themselves.

Many cultures have a code. The best working relationships were built on trust and respect. Not all the relationships resulted in friendship, but I had to build and maintain them so that I and others could perform their roles even with the people who were difficult to get along with. During my policing career, I spent a lot of time with my work colleagues, probably more than with my family, so I obviously enjoyed working with people who made it more enjoyable and who looked at things the same way I would.

I remember one winter in Alice Springs, working a night shift with my good friend, Rowan Wake. It was a typical busy night busy. Fires frequently popped up in the riverbeds, some lit by people trying to stay warm, others just to cause trouble.

We were called to a job where a group of drunks was throwing rocks and bottles at a fire in the river. Rowan and I decided to drive down to the riverbed in Charles Creek to locate the group and try to extinguish the fires. We found the group, rounded them up, and started putting them into the back of our police cage. Soon, we had about eight or nine people crammed in the back, and it got loud and chaotic. As we tried to close the door, they pushed back.

Then I saw an indigenous man with a rum bottle, shoving his way toward the cage. I turned to Rowan and said, "Just let them out. Let's see what happens."

As they exited the cage one by one, they immediately started attacking us. It was chaos as people were swinging left and right. The fire brigade showed up just in time to help. As each person took a swing, we put them to the ground. I radioed for backup – it was just me and Rowan against ten people. After a few minutes, some of the group fled while we managed to subdue the rest and throw them back into the cage. Neither of us got hit, which was incredible. The guys from NTFS were great; they gave us a much-needed hand.

The next day, Rowan and I went to the gym as usual. A few of the fire service guys and some people from the hospital were there. They were all talking about the incident, going on about how these "kung fu" moves were being pulled off in the middle of it all. Rowan and I just stood there, quietly listening and trying not to laugh. Eventually, someone asked why we were laughing, and we said, "Well, we were the ones in the river last night."

It was surreal, looking back and laughing about something that had been so intense at the time. But those were fun times that I'll never forget.

Bringing humour into a made it a lot easier to process. Obviously, it would have been inappropriate if it had involved serious injury or a fatality.

Understanding professional relationships was essential to the development of my career and reputation. I achieved that by providing a safe space for my colleagues to voice their opinions without any judgement because I always respected someone else's opinion even if it was different to my own. When people saw that my police patrol group was working well together, more people wanted to work under my leadership not because of me personally but as a group of people who were innovative and had good morale.

I enjoyed working in a team environment with various backgrounds and cultures but we were all equal. I was the sergeant in charge, but I always maintained where I came from. I showed that I was always one to be counted on in their time of need, much like my children expected me to be.

Having good working relationships throughout my different careers has enabled me more freedom to spend positive energy on important relationships and less time focusing on the negative. The time I spent as a plumber was enjoyable because of great working relationships. I learned by not leaning into a relationship that wasn't important to the other person. Every interaction I have with someone I want to show them that they are my focus, and they have all my attention. Building a strong professional circle within any organisation was critical to my career opportunities starting to come my way.

As previously discussed, I wanted my working relationships to have trust, respect, open communication, inclusion and self-awareness.

When mutual respect became the foundation of my inner circle, it created a safe space for honest and open conversations to take place. This mutual respect fostered an environment where everyone felt valued and heard, allowing us to discuss even the most difficult topics without fear of judgement. Over time, the honesty and trust within these relationships deepened, strengthening our bonds and helping us navigate challenges together. This growth not only enhanced our connections but also taught me the importance of respect and authenticity in building meaningful relationships.

Every problem has a solution. I knew when I was out of my depth or didn't understand a problem, I needed to be open to someone who may have a better solution. This is where the inclusion factor comes in. Just like the diversity of this great country, interacting with people from different backgrounds who have varying opinions, insights and perspectives greatly enriches my decision-making process. Each unique viewpoint provides valuable context and alternative ways of thinking, broadening my understanding of complex issues.

By embracing cultural awareness, I am not only better equipped to make more informed and inclusive decisions, but I also cultivate empathy and respect for others. This diversity encourages collaboration, innovation, and a deeper appreciation for the rich tapestry of experiences that make up our communities, ultimately enhancing both personal growth and professional effectiveness.

I spent many years working in remote indigenous communities of the Northern Territory, my reputation was built on cultural awareness and the working relationships I had with stakeholders and community elders. I learned a lot about Aboriginal culture and the dynamics of how community relationships evolved. If we look at how western society operates, it is like a pyramid approach: the leader sits on top looking over the people below and as each level gets closer to the ground, the level of responsibility decreases.

Educating myself about why Aboriginal paintings and drawings contained circles, it became evident how their structure worked. In a circle everyone is equal. Everyone can see each other and not one person above the other is an example of a harmonious community. Employing this in my professional relationships has been very helpful, that everyone has an opinion and most importantly a voice to be heard.

While I truly valued the responsibility and privilege of leading my team, I came to understand that not everything was within my control. Leadership taught me that focusing on what I can influence, my own words, actions and decisions, was far more impactful than worrying about external factors beyond my reach. By grounding myself in accountability and self-awareness, I was able to lead with integrity and inspire my team to do the same. This realisation also reinforced the importance of resilience and adaptability, enabling me to navigate challenges more effectively while fostering a culture of trust and collaboration within my team.

Back in the late 2000s working in Alice Springs, I was the Sergeant of A-watch. I had never been with a better bunch of people – hardworking, dedicated, felt like a special family, a love was there but never spoken of.

On one busy night shift, I and the other three units were 15 km south of Alice Springs dealing with an incident. I then received another call for any unit to attend an "intruders on", basically someone breaking into a house. While rapidly heading for that job, another call came to my mobile, it was from a member of my patrol group. He was working at the police station and he was screaming on the phone which was hard to understand. I told him to just calm down and speak slowly. I could hear the fear in his voice still yelling, "It's my house, it's my house, my girlfriend is home alone, she can hear him breaking in!"

My foot went down on the accelerator as I told him, "I promise I'll get there as quick as I can push this car. We are all heading there, just keep me informed of what's happening there." I drove the pants off that stock-standard Commodore and I'm sure there was smoke coming off the brake pads when I arrived.

I ran towards the house, and as I got closer, I notified all units to turn off their sirens. I didn't want the offender to know we were close. My heart rate was racing but still in control. I heard glass breaking. I kicked in the door and saw his girlfriend standing there shaking and holding a sword. She looked very pale.

I said, "We are here your safe, put the sword down." I heard someone in the back sounding like they were trying to get out the bathroom window. My colleague was fast, and I heard them scuffling, and then someone yelled out. "We got him."

My phone rang again, it was the frantic member crying on the phone. He just kept saying "Thank you" repeatedly, so I just listened and told him that it was ok. He arrived shortly after, gave him a big hug, and told him that there was no need to thank me. I miss the camaraderie of my former working relationships. I spent more time with them than my family. One consistent thing was that we picked each other up when things really hit the fan.

In critical situations, I could visibly see the shift in facial expressions as stress levels rose among those I was responsible for protecting. It was clear that not everyone could suppress their feelings or prevent their emotions from bubbling to the surface. Recognising these signs taught me the importance of emotional awareness and the need to remain calm and composed under pressure. By acknowledging and addressing these emotions rather than ignoring them, I was better able to provide reassurance, guidance and support to those around me. This experience reinforced my belief that emotional intelligence and empathy are essential for effective leadership, especially in high-stress environments where people look to their leaders for stability and direction.

It was my duty to protect them in all my capacity and hopefully save some space for me, which I now know I failed to do. Reflecting on so many incidents I attended over the years, I wonder how they affected my colleagues, if they were dealing with the same mental health issues I encountered. Being professional was one of the main criteria I maintained with those special relationships but we are all human and the cost of life can never be underestimated. There were many occasions when I had to keep my team together and give them space to process what had happened in front of us.

Every day in the first responder world is different. No two days are the same. It was enjoyable driving from home to work because I knew the connections of the people I worked with were special, we promoted positivity when the real world clearly didn't. But there was one day when our outlook on the world deteriorated just that little more. A young disabled indigenous teenage girl was reported not breathing so another unit and I rushed to an address in the Darwin area. We arrived first and the ambulance was still on its way so we had the responsibility to save her life.

An elderly Caucasian male opened the door and directed me to where she was lying down in the lounge room. I pushed past him, checked her wrist for a pulse and listened for any breathing. Nothing, so I began CPR with another female officer continually checking to see if we had a pulse.

After a short period, two ambulance units arrived. I nevertheless continued with CPR which felt like a really long time. Her heart started again but she was still in a critical condition. Her brain had been starved of oxygen for a long time and we had to get her to hospital. Things became blurry in the room not because I was going to pass out but the speed of how we all worked together. We escorted the ambulance to the hospital, lights and sirens all the way. I met up with the female officers who attended, thanking them for their great effort and dedication to their roles. The shift continued with more incidents, just another day as a first responder.

A couple of days later, I checked the police reporting system to see if there were any updates on the young girl's condition – it was no longer with general duties, now being investigated by criminal investigations. I was reading the information and my heart sank: she had passed away in the hospital. I had been involved in many incidents like this but I'll never forget that job.

I had a great working relationship with all sections of the police force so I felt comfortable discussing matters of importance. I spoke with a crime member and asked why they had taken over the investigation. A warm feeling came over my body, my heart rate elevated and my hands got tighter as I clenched them with everything I had. I was informed that she had been raped on numerous occasions. I almost fell over with anger, my thoughts of hate for this world grew deeper as I questioned human nature.

I tried saving this poor girl, but I had no inclination that she had been suffering prior to that day. Honestly, I was glad she had passed away, not because I wanted her to no longer live but because of the treatment she had endured at the hands of someone who was supposed to care for her. It was so disgusting and vile that most people would not be able to fully understand.

I was also asked by the two female officers who attended that incident what had happened. I wanted to protect them both and not inform them about what the investigation had uncovered, but our relationship was strong and open communication was important. I told them what I had found out. I remember them well. Those relationships will never be forgotten, they will always be a part of my journey throughout my life.

In some of my more recent roles, developing connections and good working relationships with stakeholders has assisted my purpose and direction of where I focus my potential.

I found scheduling time to build relationships a turning point. Letting people know I have specific times to meet shows my desire to build a relationship. At that moment my focus will be completely on them.

Another issue I encountered, and I'm sure many others have, is the lack of positivity. First responders' careers involve a lot of work in the negative, people are never satisfied with the working conditions or some of their working relationships. Also, the media are focused more on the negative rather than the positive. I guess more people enjoy the drama that is happening to someone else. Have you ever noticed that when you encounter positive people, you gravitate towards them?

I find being positive allows me to make people feel good and I absorb that energy instead of sweating the small stuff, changing the mindset and finding positivity in everything. I rarely feel negative about anyone but I'm sure most people can imagine they become impatient, get angry and direct those negative behaviours toward others. Difficult relationships might be due to power struggles or climbing the leadership ladder, and this is quite evident in the police force.

I still believe that trust is the foundation of any good work relationship. A great work environment comes down to self-awareness and honest communication. Effective communication is key to successful projects and meaningful relationships. Building strong connections requires time, effort and emotional intelligence, including understanding my needs, listening mindfully and valuing others' perspectives.

Authenticity is a powerful tool when it comes to building professional relationships. Being true to myself fosters trust and helps others relate to me on a deeper level. The biggest step is to be vulnerable by sharing your passions and values. Showing my authenticity and relatability have an undeniable appeal, drawing people towards me.

12

Secret Sauce

I'm always learning and educating myself on all the important relationships I value. Since the time of being a young adult right through to where I stand today, I'm evaluating what qualities I need and want in an intimate relationship. (And I don't just mean sex, that's in the next chapter!)

When I pay attention to how my body reacts to my thoughts and feelings, it helps me understand what I truly want. As I grow, I see the person I'm with growing alongside me. It's all about having those special people by my side when things get tough, and that one person who's there when I need them most supporting me as I do the same for them.

For a relationship to be satisfying and fulfilling, it needs to be stimulating for both people. Some couples rely on physical intimacy, but that is not enough for real friendship to grow. I need mental and emotional stimulation too to stay interested in a relationship. I've been blessed to find someone who enjoys similar interests, passions and hobbies, and our conversations are never boring and monotonous. Rather they're something to look forward to every day. It's like time practically stops when I'm with her.

Instead of competing for what I want, I've learned that finding something we both love and can enjoy together is far more fulfilling.

Finding the most rewarding connection unexpectedly, a very special moment in my life. (Toorak College Ball, Melbourne, VIC)

I'm not an expert on intimate relationships but with years of experience, I've been able to now find the one in eight billion who suits me perfectly. She's not only an intelligent woman who is absolutely stunning inside and out, but she has the ability to make me laugh, outsmart or one-up me at some things, and yet, she also listens to my dreams and intricate ideas.

I love researching, studying and increasing my knowledge of the world – and her – by sharing podcasts and books and then having meaningful discussions. She takes my mind and intellect to as deep and special a place as she does in the bedroom. Challenging me and helping me to grow every time in her presence or from afar, I'm more attracted to this than anything else.

Every relationship requires effort, but it's up to each person to decide if that effort is worth it. When the connection is genuine, most days feel effortless and natural, making the work feel less like a chore and more like a shared commitment. But just saying that you love me isn't enough. It feels special to hear it, but there is so much more I need and so much more I want to give. Be consistent in how you show up, demonstrate a safe place even when upset, have that balance of being equal in the relationship and follow through with commitments and promises.

A few months ago, I discovered a great phone app that is basically a calendar that I can share with my partner. We both input our commitments and free time. It's a game-changer. We use this app every day. It allows us both to organise our lives together and plan special trips, dinners, time with family, and exercise.

As explored earlier, mindfulness and a holistic approach are key to better health and wellbeing. In the context of this special relationship, I've found a partner who inspires me to continually prioritise my healing and growth, making our connection a meaningful part of my journey.

Every day I realise there are moments in time that become memories. Being present in the moment and showing every ounce of focus on her when she is looking at me in conversation is so important. I know many people are busy in their lives but when I go out for dinner, my phone never comes out. It doesn't sit on the table; it's set to Do Not Disturb and I put it away. The only time my phone comes out is to take another magical photo with her, choosing her as a priority for my time, energy and behaviours.

Communication is so important, especially open conversations. Nothing is off the table with us. Being authentic and genuine, making decisions that prioritise connection over convenience.

We engage in many rituals every day. For example, I would send her a list of questions to answer and I would give my responses in return. It's a great way to gather knowledge and insight into each other. Questions can be about intimacy, family, work, life, past experiences or future aspirations. It's always evolving and lots of fun. It's important to respect each other's boundaries without judgement, however. Everyone should set and hold clear boundaries.

Learning and practising new skills to navigate hard conversations, while working together to find a solution (versus just giving up because it's too difficult), is so rewarding. But that hard work needs to be a mutual team effort to support and care for each other, while still honouring individual needs, desires and boundaries. It's critical in an intimate relationship that both people are equals and each person knows they have value. Opinions and thoughts will vary but acknowledge and validate them. Relationships should not involve power imbalances. Tolerating a lack of mutual respect and allowing repeated hurtful behaviour is dangerous. I speak from experience.

Relationships may take effort, but with the right person, every moment of care and commitment feels like a beautiful journey worth embracing. Bringing two individuals together who have their own very different lives can be challenging. Men in particular find it difficult to be vulnerable and open to new emotional connections because it feels like weakness – the truth is the exact opposite! It shows strength, wisdom and self-awareness. If I've done something wrong, I apologise wholeheartedly and take accountability for my actions. Likewise, I will always accommodate my partner's needs, helping her to feel seen, heard and valued, and creating a safe place so she is comfortable with expressing vulnerability. Of course, not every conversation goes smoothly but I would like to make sure that I approach conflict with maturity and respect her opinion even if it's different to mine.

And in resolving to accept differences, it's the simple things that matter the most, like saying "I want to make you happy" or "I want to show up better for you".

Unfortunately, the value of these words doesn't stretch much past feeling good for a fleeting moment if they aren't aligned with action. I know that my partner wants to hear how special she is to me but my behaviour must be consistent with my words. And it must be action that she appreciates. Understanding some differences between feminine and masculine traits is super helpful! I know my partner wants understanding, respect, attention, devotion, validation, reassurance and wants to be cared for (knowing she's very capable of looking after herself). As a man, I want appreciation, purpose, trust, approval, admiration, encouragement and acceptance.

Not every relationship has worked out for me, obviously. I've had girlfriends, been engaged, married and separated. I often think, *What if?* What if I could have made other choices? – better ones, different ones, easier ones, harder ones. I can't change the past, but I've learned from my experience, and I know what's important to me now and what I was looking for in that special person. When I was at my lowest point in a previous relationship, it opened my eyes to all the little mistakes, the obstacles and setbacks, the trials and errors.

They were all little pushes to where I am today. I am grateful for everything I have today, and I strive to better myself for tomorrow. Life gets better when I realise that I didn't really make a wrong decision – the choices I made led me exactly to where I'm supposed to be. If I went back and fixed all the mistakes I've ever made, I would erase myself.

The feelings I have in this present moment, knowing the best kind of love, caught me off guard and left me amazed at how it found its way into my life. It's beyond what I could have imagined, making every moment with this amazing person special.

So, don't just hope for love, embrace the unexpected, because that's where the most beautiful stories begin. Love often surprises us. It's not planned but rather stumbled upon. Instant connection, unique chemistry, and delightful surprises create the most beautiful love stories. It's about magical moments where hearts beat effortlessly.

True love often arrives unannounced, raw in its authenticity, and sparked by an undeniable connection that transcends the ordinary. It begins with an unanticipated bond and deepens over time into something profoundly meaningful, defying simple explanations and embodying the kind of story that words alone cannot fully capture.

Having a partner who is in the mood for me every day is incredible. She wants to talk to me every day, no matter how busy she is. She craves my touch and cherishes my friendship and advice. She desires my presence, and provides and protects me. There's a saying I like to tell her all the time: "The more I have of you, the more I want you."

On reflection, things fall into place when I least expect it. I realised that what was left behind was making space for what was about to arrive, and it truly did in her case. The philosophy that doors close to turn you towards ones that are opening is so true. I don't define myself by the limits of what I've known, and I never limit my potential to what others have said is possible. I make space for what I love and for what makes me feel alive.

I'm not complacent though. I will never lose the inspiration to tell my beautiful partner that I love her enough to fight for her, compromise for her and sacrifice myself for her if need be. Enough to miss her incredibly when we're apart, no matter what length of time it's for and regardless of the long distance, enough to believe in our relationship to stand by it through the worst of times, to have faith in our strength as a couple and to never give up on us. Enough to spend the rest of my life with her, be there for when she needs or wants me and never ever want to leave her or to live without her. I love her this much.

I saw an article referencing how many summers I will have during my life on this planet. Most people average around 80 summers, more if your health and wellbeing are good. So, after the age of 50 years old, looking at the next chapter of summers, I want to share them with someone magical. I have the mindset to never hold back now.

I'm all in, completely and unconditionally. I will share my heart and every part of my soul with her, letting her know that while I may not have much to offer, my love will always be whole. I promise I will never half love her, she will have all of me, always.

When I'm in a relationship, people have their opinions, good or bad. I've even met people trying to break up other people's relationships. So how to keep a relationship? How to ignore the opinions? Always communicate; talk about things. The good and bad build trust. Be honest, be faithful and be there for one another. Leave the past in the past. Know that having arguments is normal, know that I won't always be happy. Don't expect change, appreciate the flaws, appreciate each other, become best friends, and love each other unconditionally.

In my opinion, if someone expresses how they need to be loved and the other person feels it would be burdensome or that they are asking too much, then that's not the person for you. I want someone who values me and will want to learn and grow with me. Love takes compromise and it requires us both to do what's needed to make each other feel safe and secure in the relationship.

After 50 years, when you least expected things to fall into place, you realise that what was left behind was making space for what was about to arrive. The quiet let me hear the guidance; the unhappiness in previous relationships forced me to make a move. The unsettledness made me keep seeking a new beginning, the doors closed to the ones that were opening. The lessons were always leading me every time I got it wrong. Always with the belief I was one step closer to getting it right. Everything encountered throughout my life has put me in a position that gave me hope to allow my life to be bigger than I ever thought it could be. Being so vulnerable to embody more beauty than I ever thought possible.

Many people think that intimacy is about sleeping together but true intimacy goes far beyond the physical; it's about sharing my deepest fears, insecurities and vulnerabilities with someone who embraces me without judgement. Someone who holds my heart gently in their hands. Real intimacy is when I can open my innermost thoughts, my past and my trauma, to another person knowing that they will listen with empathy and understanding. When I'm totally comfortable, I can reveal the broken pieces of my soul, and my amazing partner responds with kindness and love.

Intimacy is when I find a haven in her presence. A place where I can be my authentic self without fear of rejection. It's when I can stand in front of her, stripped of pretence, and I am reassured with those magical words, "You're safe with me." I know she's the one who will stand by my side and who will remind me that I'm never alone on this beautiful and sometimes challenging journey.

The truth is that the more intimately you know someone, the more clearly you see their flaws. That's why marriages fail, why children are abandoned, why friendships don't last. Maybe consider how you love someone when you see the way they act when they're broke, under pressure or hungry. Love is something different. Love is choosing to serve someone despite their heart or circumstance. Love is patient and kind. Love is deliberate. Love is hard.

It takes work to maintain an incredibly intimate relationship. My advice? Focus on the details. Simple things mean bigger things. A kiss hello or a kiss goodbye. Ask how your partner's day was, help with daily tasks and not for anything in return but to show investment in the relationship. Take some time out each day for deep conversation: share your thoughts, ideas, dreams and future vision. Also, listen and validate theirs.

Time together and time alone is important. Intimate relationships are perhaps the most fertile ground for inner evolutionary work and healing. Both time together and time alone are essential in any relationship. Intimate relationships often provide the richest opportunities for personal growth and healing, as they tend to bring out our deepest fears and insecurities. These moments of vulnerability can serve as powerful catalysts for self-discovery and emotional evolution.

I know when my relationship is going better than ever because I wait impatiently for the next deep and meaningful conversation whilst having lots of fun sharing inside jokes and experiences. I would like everyone to have a great relationship – they are a game changer for our mental health and overall quality of life.

Finding this type of relationship is a conscious and deliberate decision that requires us to become aware of our past choices. It's also a decision to challenge our limiting beliefs about our worth and what we think we deserve. It's like a war cry – the longer I continue to settle for less, the longer it is until I receive what I truly deserve. It's not always about the search. Many people are already in a fantastic relationship, but this is a gentle reminder to hold on tight and keep doing the work you no doubt did in the beginning. A healthy relationship requires a decision and commitment from both individuals to actively put in the effort required to show up in the way that's needed each and every day.

Falling in love with someone who enjoys me being my authentic self, who celebrates my quirks and imperfections, and who doesn't criticise me is so refreshing. We only have a short period of time on this planet and I intend to spend it with someone who lifts me up, supports my dreams and loves me for who I truly am. Every relationship I've had has meaning and purpose, but it is up to me to absorb the knowledge and gain value from them. Without them, I wouldn't be the amazing person I am today.

13

Nitty Gritty

Let's get to the nitty gritty stuff that makes the juices flow and my heart race. I've been in love a few times and experienced many different things – what I thought it should look like and the reality of how it was.

I was told that I was likely to fall in love three times during my life. My first love happened when I was quite young; I still remember her, with no experience of what love was and we grew apart over something trivial.

My second love was more complex, tougher, demanding, rewarding and challenging. I learned a lot about what love is, what I enjoyed about being me and also what I disliked about myself. Through that experience, I became more precise about what I wanted, or rather, what I deserved.

Then my third love came into my life so unexpectedly that it caught me off-guard. The walls I had built around my heart and soul began breaking down just being in her presence. I suddenly felt myself deeply caring for this magical person I could never have imagined.

This kind of love makes me feel like I could never love like this again. It's the kind of love where we've become best friends but could never just be friends. When I look at her, I know she entered my life at the right time. It's the kind of love that is once in a lifetime and could never end. It's the kind of love that I've seen in movies or only in dreams and fantasies. Sometimes, when I'm alone at night I think it's the kind of love that makes me question reality, but I realise it has to be because when our eyes meet that's all I feel.

The most amazing woman in the world: there aren't enough words in existence to describe how beautiful she is.

She calms me and makes everything feel centred.

It feels like I've waited over 50 years for this person who gets me. Like I mean she *really* gets me like no one else ever has. Our connection on so many intricate levels is incomparable. I found friendship, a lover and my soulmate wrapped up in the prettiest little package; truly remarkable and unforgettable. Experiencing the fierce and unwavering love she gives me is nothing short of incredible. Her love resonates deep within me, grounding me in every moment of this journey. For the first time, I feel truly whole in a way I never have before.

Everything happens for a reason. My happiest moments, the most painful failures and my successes are all from the experiences I've had and the knowledge I've gained. And in learning to pay attention to everything and everyone around me, I've understood that I can't truly love anyone else until I love myself first.

I remember the first time we met and how unexpectedly my life changed. I didn't see it coming but it was like fate brought us together. I'm thankful to her for making me realise that I deserve to be loved and happy.

I am truly grateful for every moment we share. She inspires me daily to be my best, and the way she holds my hand so tightly reassures me that she'll always be there.

Recently, I read *The Five Love Languages* by Gary Chapman, which explores how people give and receive love in unique ways. Chapman describes these "languages" as words of affirmation, quality time, physical touch, acts of service, and receiving gifts. Learning each other's love language has deepened our connection, helping us both feel genuinely appreciated and understood.

Words of affirmation – When this is someone's primary love language, they enjoy kind words and encouragement, uplifting quotes, love notes and cute text messages. You can make this person's day by complimenting them or pointing out what they do well.

Quality time – This love language values your full presence when you are together. They feel most loved if you give them your undivided attention. This means putting down the mobile phone, turning off the computer, making eye contact, thoughtfully interacting and actively listening. People with this love language are looking for quality over quantity.

Physical touch – A person with physical touch as their primary love language feels love through physical affection. Aside from sex, they feel loved when their partner holds their hand, touches their arm or gives them a massage. This person's idea of a wonderful date night might be cuddling on the couch while watching a movie, slow dancing together with a lot of physical contact, or taking a long walk together while holding hands. They feel most loved when physically interacting with their partner.

Acts of service – Those who prefer this language feel loved and appreciated through acts such as helping with the dishes, running errands and putting fuel in the car. If an individual's main love language is acts of service, then they'll notice and appreciate the little things done for them. They tend to perform acts of service and kindness for others too.

Receiving gifts – For someone who resonates with this love language, gifts symbolise love, care and affection. They treasure not only the gift itself but also the time and effort the giver put into it. They do not necessarily expect large or expensive presents; it's the effort and thoughtfulness behind the gift that count. People with this love language can often remember every little gift they have received from their loved ones because it makes such an impact on them.

Something I practise every day in my relationship is to give her a big hug and hold it for at least eight seconds or more. It has been scientifically proven that holding someone releases dopamine in the brain which gives the feeling of connection and belonging.

I'm sure most people can reflect on previous relationships and remember what they did to attract another person, to win them over and while dating. Unfortunately, it's often forgotten once you're married. Sadly, that urge to try different things, the drive to continually win over your partner is lost, and you become complacent. Then one day the happiness in your life is cut short as you realise you've compromised how you're treated for the sake of their happiness.

In *Way of the Peaceful Warrior* by Dan Millman, the character Socrates said, "When you like a flower, you just pluck it. But when you love a flower, you water it daily."

I'm amazed by the insight and wisdom he possessed. It's such a simple statement, yet so powerful. The importance of being open and leaning into our relationship is vital to me. I want us to grow together, constantly learning about each other but also recognise and support each other's individual growth. It's funny how now the simple things I do become bigger moments and memories; for example, opening the door for her, watching out for her when traffic approaches while walking, getting her flowers for no reason but to show I love her (and because I know she loves flowers).

I can't stress the importance of sharing how I feel. I want her to know I'll wait for her because honestly, I don't want anyone else. Every moment we spend apart only strengthens my resolve, reminding me of how deeply I cherish and need her in my lifetime. Time may pass and circumstances may change but my feelings for her will remain constant and unwavering.

She is the one I dream about, the one who completes my world. I want her to know that I don't want to settle for anything less than the extraordinary we share in every heartbeat. When I say she's the only one I want now and always, it's true. I want everyone to know this person who makes her feelings obvious to the world, who invites me into her family, who holds my hand in public, and kisses me in the gym so everyone knows we are taken. I want to make plans with her and explore the world. I miss her when she's not around. I will always ask her what the best things are about her day, and she in turn cares about my day too. I deserve someone who gives me strength, someone who gives me courage, and that person is her.

Never stop telling someone "I love you". It's only three words but they hold so much meaning. I always need to follow it up with action too, because in relationships people can say anything but I believe you also need to show it.

I love just sitting with her in silence listening and watching her. I'm mesmerised by her beautiful voice, her elegant beauty. I enjoy just laughing with her and want to show her things and share things with her. I want to explore her magnificent mind; I want to study and explore her wonderful body. Just holding her in my arms I found everything I wanted. She is beautiful, giving, gentle, idiotically and deliciously feminine. I never thought that after the age of fifty, one could get so completely besotted with another person that a minute away from them felt like a thousand years.

According to John Eldredge in his book *Wild at Heart* which discusses masculinity:

> If you get the chance to love another woman or man like they deserve, show them a love that doesn't leave. Let your actions complement the beauty of their soul. Be the man she so desperately seeks, and she will lead you to a place within yourself that you have always searched for.

I've come to realise the importance of previous relationships in showing me what is truly important, and I've realised that the honeymoon phase never ends with the right person. When I'm in a strong relationship, I can grow closer and fall more in love even in the hard times. I think the greatest joy is that I found somebody who opens my eyes, makes me a better person and inspires me to do better things with my life. That's a great gift and a great love.

> The wrong man in your life will teach you that you can do it all by yourself. The right man will know you can but will not let you. He will stand by your side, share the load and assist you in thriving together.
>
> **– Chris Perry**

If I could have every single inch of her body pressed tight against mine, I would still say pull me closer. I love planning trips away for a night or over several days, just so we can be together. Asking her to come lay with me for hours so we can talk thousands of nothings while it means millions of something. Finding a person who wants to experience life and all it has to offer is really rewarding and fun. Those intimate moments are like everlasting memories we continue to build.

I crave her in the most innocent form. It's not just the physical attraction to each other but I want to show her she has a safe place to be herself. I love giving her forehead kisses just to say that I adore her. Having a calm connection to the everyday moments where we just exist together. It's about holding her hand, sharing a smile and knowing we have each other. That's all I ever want.

The conversations we have are like nothing else I've ever experienced. No subject or topic is off-limits. We have managed to create a safe place with each other where no judgement exists. We can just be ourselves completely in a world full of noise. Her words resonate deeply with me and every thoughtful action she takes, every piece of wisdom she shares, brings light into my life. To find a beautiful mind always so considerate and insightful is wonderful.

Our conversations are moments I'll never forget. I hope she knows just how much she means to me and how much her presence and support enrich my life. I feel truly appreciated by her, as I appreciate her.

I want to ask her if I could have experienced this with anyone, I'm grateful it was her. She has shown me what it means to be appreciated, wanted and above all loved. It sounds clichéd but you had me at hello! I remember our first conversation and how my heart raced, and my cheeks flushed. Then finally meeting was a day I'll never forget. The universe saw me struggling and said, "Here's the sweetest, most patient person you could ever ask for. She will keep your heart safe." Sometimes all it takes is for a woman who was never loved properly to meet the man who was never appreciated and then it all starts to make sense. All that love eventually leads to a build-up of physical desire. Of course, I've had sexual relationships before, like my partner has, but this time it's different.

This time I've connected on so many levels. The desire, the need to please her constantly, to want to study her mind and her body as we both gain knowledge and empower each other to explore and enjoy each other's company is intense. I've not mastered the art of having sex – I'm no expert – but I will continue to explore my sexual desires and now I have an amazing woman who also loves the adventure of our journey together.

> Sex is an important aspect of many relationships and while research finds that while regular sex does help to cement a couple's emotional bond, that boost doesn't derive from the physical act as much as from what it expresses – openness, transparency, positive communication, and a commitment to foster and maintain erotic energy.[23]

I enjoy watching her response to emotions and her sexual appetite. People say being a great lover all comes down to technique. That is important but there is so much more. I need to listen to her cues, her moves, the sounds she makes.

Communication is such an important instrument during intimate moments together. It's a lot about the build-up, the anticipation of what may happen. Never underestimate the power of messaging each other while at work or at home when you're not in her presence! As humans, we crave physical touch. Being flirtatious with her just to keep her simmering through the day, teasing her, not allowing those feelings to go cold, and making her want me is highly erotic. I enjoy sexting with her. I never know what's going to pop up on my phone! I want her in the right headspace knowing soon enough she will feel euphoric, sexy and satisfied. Open discussions on what each other likes or wants to explore creates great sexual tension, if I find something hot, she likes to lean into it and vice versa.

Enjoying each other's company both sexually and emotionally is an amazing experience, as long as there is trust and respect. As I've said previously, I never stop learning and it's the same with sexual experiences. I keep pushing myself to try things I haven't tried before. I am committed to improving my sexual intelligence!

---

23 - Psychology Today, "Love and Sex", viewed Jan 2025, https://www.psychologytoday.com/intl/basics/relationships/love-and-sex

Sexual intelligence is about understanding and navigating your own and others' feelings, boundaries and needs when it comes to intimacy, making sure both people feel valued and safe. Communication plays a big role too being able to talk openly about desires, preferences, and concerns without fear or judgement can strengthen a connection.

It's also important to have the right knowledge about sexual health, anatomy and consent, so you can approach things with confidence and care. Beyond the physical side, sexual intelligence is about managing emotions like vulnerability or insecurity and creating an environment of trust. At its core, it is not just about sex, it is about building meaningful, respectful relationships that make both people feel understood and supported. By combining honesty, respect and emotional understanding, sexual intelligence helps create deeper connections and more fulfilling experiences for everyone involved.

Mental and physical health play a big part in the bedroom. Looking after both these areas is key to becoming a great lover. If I'm not being mindful of my mental health, considering my stress levels or being aware of negative self-talk and judgement, my head won't allow me to be present in the moment. Medications too can affect performance in the bedroom.

> The popular medications known as selective serotonin reuptake inhibitors, or SSRIs, can help lift people out from under a dark cloud of depression. But there are some side effects from antidepressants, including those that can affect your sex life.
>
> In addition to reducing interest in sex, SSRI medications can make it difficult to become aroused, sustain arousal, and reach orgasm. Some people taking SSRIs can't

have an orgasm at all. These symptoms tend to become more common with age.

SSRI medications include:

- citalopram (Celexa)
- escitalopram (Lexapro)
- fluoxetine (Prozac)
- fluvoxamine (Luvox)
- paroxetine (Paxil)
- sertraline (Zoloft)
- vortioxetine (Trintellix, formerly called Brintellix).[24]

I work on my physical health rigorously. I want to maintain my fitness and strength as I get older. My body must get me to the finish line, so I need to eat properly and sleep well. There is a lot of clinical research available about the benefits of maintaining mental and physical health that assists with positive factors like blood flow for arousal, erections and a female's vulva sensitivity. I want to look after myself and I know my partner does too. Being healthy makes us great lovers because we are on the same level and understand the importance of great sex.

Most people live in their heads when having sex and are not truly present. It took decades to finally have the best sex of my life! Relating to my body allows me to really connect with my partner. We recently attended a massage course in Byron Bay and learned the art of touch: sixteen hours of massaging our bodies, not in a sexual way but understanding what it really felt like to connect to another

---

24 - LeWine HE. "Sexual side effects of SSRIs: Why it happens and what to do Coping with this common side effect from antidepressants" *Havard Health Publishing.* 2023 Jul 7. https://www.health.harvard.edu/womens-health/when-an-ssri-medication-impacts-your-sex-life

person on a deeper level. Learning how to slow everything down was such an important factor. And it wasn't just the use of my hands; I incorporated all my arms. The key was to never lose touch with her body, covered in oil, all slippery, sensual and very aroused. I highly recommend any couple wanting to explore how they can really connect on a different level to attend a course like the one we did.

Great sex is about enjoying the moment, the feeling and being free to explore each other enjoying sensations and pleasure. Having a relationship that we are connected to on so many levels promotes confidence in each other. She knows that I love her body, and I definitely know she loves mine. That self-acceptance around my entire being, when she looks at my body, my genitals and feels excited like I do, builds so much confidence in each other that there's no judgement. I enjoy the pleasure that she provides for me and I know she loves the pleasure she receives.

I want to always pay attention to her needs and cues. I carefully examine what she likes, and I lean into it. Great sex happens when there is a balance between receiving and giving. Like making a masterpiece, we approach our love life to make every experience memorable and amazing. So, there are times we like to push the boundaries … you just never know what each other has in mind. Importantly we always talk about boundaries and reading each other's body language. Turning up the heat in the bedroom, trying something kinky like being tied up to a bed frame is incredibly sexy. I was always bondage curious. It's something everybody should try, when one person has relinquished their power of movement while the other maintains control. It brings a sense of relaxation that my partner has taken control and is driving the narrative, but it's also a feeling of heightened sensitivity because I never know what's going to happen next. It also builds a lot of trust in my partner. Basically, she is controlling my whole body which is highly intimate.

If being tied up isn't your thing, something else that may tickle your fancy is temperature and texture play. Being blindfolded and having your ability to move taken away means your senses are super heightened when touched with different textures like a feather or an ice cube or some hot melted wax being dripped onto your body. Some people may say "not for me" and that's ok. Just communicate with your partner what you would like to try or leave it for another time.

I didn't realise that my testosterone levels were the highest in the morning. I love morning sex! There is nothing better than spooning my naked partner throughout the whole night and waking up together in each other's arms. According to Dr Helen Fisher in *Why We Love*:

> Why not start any day off with a bang since orgasm releases dopamine, a brain cognition booster. Morning sex orgasms give me oxytocin, the "cuddle" hormone that helps me feel loving and bonded and helps my partner's oestrogen, which builds collagen in the skin and endorphins, which relieve pain naturally and boost your mood.

If morning love is never planned, I want her to be dreaming about it during the night, indulging in her erotic imagination and building anticipation for that sexual tension in the morning. Or I want to have a shower with her just to get ourselves ready for the day. Importantly, I feel comfortable discussing anything, no matter how "taboo", sharing fantasies and then creating them together while letting her know how arousing it can be for her too.

It's not just the act of having sex but what happens after sex that is also very important. My body's reaction to the amazing connection with my partner, the sexual "afterglow", is necessary to remain connected. I love cuddling and enjoying the conversations. Some people just want to go to sleep which is fine but the feeling of enhanced sexual satisfaction following a sexual experience makes us both feel better about each other for days.

> I love how sensual we are in bed. I've been thinking about how hot it would be for you to blindfold me. If I can't see you, I'll be able to feel your touch on my body even more strongly. Do you want to try it?[25]

I didn't realise until I conducted my own research that over 80% of women can't reach orgasm through penetration alone, so many women must feel no satisfaction in their sex lives. It is easy for the man to worry more about their own orgasm and not care so much about the satisfaction of their partner. So, mastering new skills is a must in this area. Discovering the female anatomy, exploring every millimetre, will keep any man in good stead. All I want to achieve is pleasure for my partner first then I'm happy to follow. Locating her nerve endings that are tucked away is key! A message for the guys: there is more than one spot to attend to, which is why it's crucial to stimulate properly.

We are all human and have sexual ideas that excite us but most of the time, we think in terms of the specific behaviours underneath them. It's an interesting window into individual erotic psychology and why we crave the things we want.

---

25 - Cunov K. "The Difference Between Pleasure, Sensual, Sexual & Erotic – and Why It Matters", 2020 Dec 22. https://kendracunov.com/2020/12/22/the-difference-between-pleasure-sensual-sexual-erotic-and-why-it-matters/

14

Growing Your Tool Kit

At this time in my journey, the focus is to never stop learning and continue expanding my knowledge about how to look after myself, my family and my friends. Improving connections expands my mind to be open to different opportunities and experiences.

Looking back to the time as a licensed tradesman, it was critical to have the right tools for any job, to overcome any issue or obstacle when they appeared. Using the same analogy for my mental and physical health, I needed to expand my mental toolbox to give me the options to look after myself.

I've developed the mindset to be very open to exploring new ways of looking after my mental health and passing what I have learned to others. If I just sat there on my lounge chair over the past 10 years feeling sorry for myself, my life would be a different story right now. Why should I limit myself to a life of taking prescribed medication, masking what's really going on inside my mind? Recovery is possible, it's hard work and takes time, possibly years of dedication, but you can do it.

The average lifetime for a human being is approximately 82 years. I'm currently 50 years old, I feel healthy physically and mentally. I can always continue to improve my mental and physical health, potentially increasing my time on this planet. If I were to think about in more depth what it means to me, I would consider that I've enjoyed 50 summers in my life and if I continue to look after myself, I'll be able to see over another 30 summers.

*Leaving footprints in the sand: reflecting how far I've come on my journey.
(Lakes Entrance, VIC)*

Through many years of researching and figuring out what coping strategies were the best for me, I had to prioritise time with a structured approach.

Developing a personal mental health toolkit has been a trans-formative process, equipping me with the skills, resources and coping strategies to navigate life's challenges and improve my mental wellbeing. It begins with self-awareness, understanding my triggers, recognising patterns and reflecting on what keeps me balanced and grounded. From there, I've built core coping strategies, such as regular exercise, healthy eating and mindfulness practices.

Problem-solving skills are another crucial component. Breaking down challenges into manageable steps and focusing on what I can control has helped me approach obstacles with clarity and confidence. Equally important is building a strong support network of friends, family, mentors, or professionals who provide emotional support and guidance when needed. I also leverage practical resources, such as mindfulness apps, mental health books and local support programs.

Maintaining this toolkit requires regular check-ins with myself to assess my mental health and adjust my strategies as life changes. By prioritising these practices, I've become more prepared to face obstacles and embrace opportunities, knowing I have the tools to support myself through life's ups and downs. This intentional approach ensures I'm actively fostering resilience and wellbeing every day.

I've tried to implement different mottos in my life, "not worrying about the things that are not in my control, just concentrating on what's in my control". It has alleviated a lot of stress, and I've become more focused on positive outcomes.

Below is a list of items to consider including in one's personal toolkit. The list is not extensive but they are things that I have tried.

- Therapy
- Journaling
- Meditation
- Positive affirmations

- Mindfulness
- Light meditation
- Chakras
- Muscle relaxation
- Breath work
- Water immersion
- Floatation tanks
- Safe place Mornington
- Tremor work
- Yoga
- Pilates
- Gym work
- Walking in nature
- Relaxation techniques
- Nutrition
- Detoxification
- Spiritual/Religious activities
- Community therapy
- CBT
- REBT
- Gestalt
- Emotional focus therapy
- Art therapy
- EMDR
- Neuropsychotherapy
- Horse Therapy
- Swimming
- Surfing

What works for me may not work for others, so the toolbox will vary from person to person. So, naturally, the tools will vary. When looking at myself as a whole person, my values, characteristics and personality play a role in what types of strategies I relate to the most. I like a combination of goal-oriented coping strategies and intuitive practices.

I need to be adaptive and fluid in my approach to my health. Strategies I tried previously may no longer work so I need to mix things up as I continue to grow and change. Try standing in front of the mirror in the bathroom, look at the person staring back and ask, "What are my biggest mental health needs?" Reflection is an amazing tool in deciding what to put in a mental health tool kit, reflecting on where I've struggled, what could I've done better and what skills was I lacking.

Journaling is an incredible tool. According to that research (Smyth et al., 2018; Koziol, 2021), journaling may help ease our distress when we're struggling. People who journaled saw the biggest reduction in symptoms like depression, anxiety, and hostility, particularly if they were very distressed to begin with. It's cathartic to write my thoughts down. It cultivates a greater sense of meaning as well as improving my mental health. Every week I look back at my journal to see any thought patterns, this reveals what sort of mental health tools I require. Clarifying my thoughts and becoming more objective, it is easy to go back to what I wrote a few hours, days, or weeks before and distinguish between reality and my feelings. So, what areas of the brain do we use for journaling?

> The left hemisphere, more specifically Broca's area, is associated with speech production and articulation. Our ability to articulate ideas, as well as use words

accurately in spoken and written language, has been attributed to this crucial area. With its help, we already start to express in words what we feel and what we think. Our limbic system, specifically our amygdala, is responsible for processing our emotions, and which triggers our fight/flight/freeze reactions under fear, anxiety, threats or stress. When we start writing and processing those emotions, the amygdala "calms down" a little ("name it to tame it"). As journaling becomes a habit, our amygdala becomes calmer and calmer. That is because we start to understand better the emotions we experience, so we don't experience them anymore at the same intensity as before. We also stop perceiving our imagined threats as being real.[26]

When I'm developing my toolbox, I go with whatever feels intuitive and helpful, thinking of things I have access to with the least number of obstacles. Sometimes the simplest ideas are often the best, especially if I am struggling badly. My tool kit is constantly evolving, and I need to work on it consistently. Every couple of months, I do a quick check to make sure the items in my tool kit are still relevant to my current needs. If I feel like my current tools aren't working for me anymore, I need to have the ability to adapt and change accordingly.

Not every day is good, and reflecting on my journey, I realise that rising stress and self-criticism weren't just internal struggles but also reactions to the external world. Life's big changes like career shifts, moving or relationship breakups taught me to redefine what "normal" means and focus on better self-care and coping strategies.

---

26 - Riès SK, Dronkers NF, Knight RT. "Choosing words: left hemisphere, right hemisphere, or both? Perspective on the lateralization of word retrieval" *Ann NY Acad Sci.* 2016 Apr;1369(1):111-31. doi: 10.1111/nyas.12993

My needs are different to what they were 20 years ago. Every day is a new chapter in my life, and nothing has been written yet. The main thing is that I believe in myself, the belief I have for a capacity to thrive despite circumstances. I'm in control of the quality of thoughts I put in my head, no one else controls that. Setting meaningful goals in line with my values and regaining a sense of purpose and direction with actionable coping skills. Some things to consider when developing a personal mental health tool kit:

- Identify recovery goals that are appropriate.
- Identify meaningful activities that are great to do.
- Build and maintain healthy relationships.
- Locate and list resources in the community that would be advantageous.
- Identify current gaps with their corresponding coping skills, and where to get help.
- Identify supports when struggling with anxiety and depressive symptoms.

In recent months, I've gathered more knowledge about a strength-based approach to looking at personal physical and mental health, remembering to always focus on my strengths and be aware of my weaknesses. This helps me build more confidence in overcoming adversity.

I've learned that prioritising emotional wellness and embracing a growth mindset helps me better understand myself, both physically and mentally. Life's challenges are inevitable, but I rely on my mental health toolkit to navigate tough times and find clarity.

After years of struggling with sleep, I've trained my mind to let go of late-night worries – now, getting over six hours of rest has transformed my mental and physical health.

Eating well and staying active makes me feel incredible, and I continue to invest in my body every day to ensure I can enjoy life for decades to come.

Some people get caught up in how difficult it is to take time out for mental and physical health. Compare it to having a shower or brushing one's teeth; that time spent on body hygiene can also be spent on brain hygiene.

I can't solve every obstacle or stress at that present time by being kind to myself and allowing sufficient time to process what is the right course of action to take. As Bishop Desmond Tutu wisely said, "How do you eat an elephant? One bite at a time." Small steps add up, and tackling issues early prevents them from becoming overwhelming and draining.

Daily check-ins with myself have become essential for mental maintenance and prevention. Over time, I've developed skills to manage emotions, prevent overwhelm, and fully appreciate life's moments. Prioritising mental wellbeing helps me stay present, recognise when others are struggling, and start meaningful conversations. Practising empathy allows me to connect with and support those around me, aiming to be a positive influence every day.

The urgent connection being more entwined with my inner world and having the ability to really understand my thoughts and feelings, as well as being able to communicate them effectively to others improves both my personal and professional relationships.

Listing priorities in my mental health toolbox is essential for me, it's the simple things that make the greatest difference. Checking in with myself, focus on the positive things in my life, and try not to be negative about things that aren't in my control. I can't change them so no point wasting energy on them.

I advocate for everyone to be kind to themselves, for many years I was very judgemental about myself, my capabilities and how the world perceived me. Practising non-judgemental awareness has changed how my thoughts come and go.

Practising Daily Mindfulness

Mindfulness has become an essential tool in my mental health toolbox. By dedicating time each day to practising mindfulness, I've learned to focus on the present moment, free from judgement or distraction. This daily habit helps me stay grounded and enhances my ability to manage stress and overwhelming emotions.

Incorporating Meditation into My Routine

Meditation is a cornerstone of my mental wellbeing strategy. Setting aside even a few minutes each day to meditate allows me to clear my mind, reduce stress, and connect with my inner self. This practice has given me greater clarity and a deeper understanding of my thoughts and feelings, helping me approach challenges with calm and focus.

Pausing Throughout the Day

Taking deliberate pauses during my day is another critical technique. Whether it's stepping outside for fresh air, closing my eyes for a moment of stillness, or simply breathing deeply, these intentional breaks allow me to reset and recharge. These pauses are small but powerful ways to maintain emotional balance.

Prioritising Self-Care

Choosing to do something for myself every day has been transformative. Whether it's engaging in a hobby, reading, or enjoying quiet time, these moments of self-care remind me to prioritise my own wellbeing. This focus on "me-time" ensures that I'm better equipped to handle the demands of daily life.

Gaining Insight through Reflection

By consistently practising mindfulness and meditation, I've developed greater insight into my thoughts and emotions. This heightened awareness helps me identify patterns, understand triggers, and respond more thoughtfully to situations. It's not just about managing emotions but also about truly understanding myself on a deeper level.

By incorporating these techniques into my daily routine, I've found a sense of emotional balance and clarity that has positively impacted every area of my life. These practices have become indispensable tools for maintaining my mental well-being and fostering a deeper connection with myself.

Grounding

Grounding, also known as Earthing, is a therapeutic practice that involves reconnecting with the earth's electrical energy by engaging in activities that create a direct physical connection with the ground. The concept is based on earthing science and grounding physics, which suggest that the earth's electrical charges can have a positive impact on the body. It's important to note that this type of grounding differs from the mental health technique used to manage stress and anxiety.

Several studies have explored the health benefits of grounding. In one such study (Chevalier et al., 2012), blood samples were taken before and after grounding to assess changes in red blood cell fluidity, which is crucial for cardiovascular health. The findings showed a significant reduction in red blood cell clumping post-grounding, indicating potential cardiovascular benefits.

Other research (Oschman et al., 2015) looked into the effects of grounding on post-exercise muscle damage. Using grounding patches and mats, researchers measured creatine kinase levels, white blood cell counts, and pain levels before and after grounding. The results suggested that grounding reduced muscle damage and pain, implying that this practice could enhance the body's healing processes. According to a review article by S.T. Sinatra et al:

> Grounding or earthing the body is having direct contact with the natural electric charge of the earth (electrons). We believe this natural anti-inflammatory is the non-pharmaceutical therapy of choice. It is free, easy to implement, and improves quality of living. Our research group refers to grounding as perhaps vitamin G or electronic nutrition. This energetic phenomenon includes the Schumann resonances, an electromagnetic "vibration" (7.83 Hz, fundamental frequency) in the atmosphere as well as a humming of the energetic surface of the earth. The Schumann resonances are not uniform but vary from moment to moment in a rhythm that affects the motion of the electrons in the surface of the earth. Thus, the earth's ground is electronically active and dynamic.[27]

---

27 - Sinatra ST, Sinatra DS, Sinatra SW, Chevalier G. "Grounding – The universal anti-inflammatory remedy" *Biomed J.* 2023 Feb;46(1):11-16. doi: 10.1016/j.bj.2022.12.002

I've incorporated grounding techniques into my daily routine, simply by stepping outside to feel the natural sunlight and walking barefoot on grass or sand. It's a small practice that helps me feel connected and recharged.

I was once advised to avoid too much salt for the sake of my arteries, but I've since come across research that presents arguments both for reducing and increasing salt intake, depending on lifestyle factors. Balance and personal context are key when making health decisions like these.

> FSANZ estimates that Australians aged two years and older eat an average of 2,150 mg of sodium per day from an average of 5,500 mg of salt (5.5 g). About 80 percent of this would be from processed foods and 20 percent from salt used at the table or in home cooking. This estimate of sodium intake from salt does not include the smaller amounts of sodium coming from naturally occurring sodium or sodium-containing food additives. Because this is an average, there will be a lot of Australians who eat more than this and more than the recommended maximum intakes.
>
> Foods that contribute the most to Australians' salt consumption are bread and bread rolls, meat, poultry and game products, including processed meat, and cereal products and cereal-based dishes such as biscuits and pizza.[28]

Every morning, I start my day by drinking a glass of water with lemon juice, cinnamon and sea salt. Baja Gold salt is considered one of the best salts for the human

---

28 - Food Standards Australia New Zealand (FSANZ), "How much sodium do Australians eat?", viewed Jan 2025, https://www.foodstandards.gov.au/consumer/nutrition/sodium-salt/salthowmuch

body. According to Gary Brecka[29], a human biology and neuroscience expert, Baja Gold contains 91 trace minerals, is tested to be free of harmful microplastics and glyphosates, and only 75% of it is sodium – the rest is made up of beneficial minerals. While pink Himalayan Sea salt has been popular, it has recently come under scrutiny due to reports of heavy metal contamination, especially from sources in China. In terms of quality, Baja Gold ranks highest, followed by Celtic salt, and pink Himalayan Sea salt is decent but not ideal.

Developing a morning routine that incorporates natural elements like sunlight, grounding, breathwork and cold showers has been transformative for me. We receive three vital things from Mother Nature: magnetism from the Earth, oxygen from the air and light from the sun. However, as a society, we've moved away from these natural sources, spending 97% of our time indoors when we're meant to be outdoors for most of our lives. The further we distance ourselves from nature, the more it impacts our health.

Gauss Law

> The total of the electric flux out of a closed surface is equal to the charge enclosed divided by the permittivity. The electric flux through an area is defined as the electric field multiplied by the area of the surface projected in a plane perpendicular to the field.[30]

Most of us aren't getting enough sun exposure. Contrary to popular belief, it's not over-exposure that's driving

---

29 - "Gary Brecka's Recommended Salt | Baha Gold Sea Salt", 2024 Mar 7, YouTube, Brecka G. https://www.youtube.com/watch?v=mAaSgTMK85w

30 - HyperPhysics (Georgia State University), "Gauss's Law", viewed Jan 2025, http://hyperphysics.phy-astr.gsu.edu/hbase/electric/gaulaw.html

issues like rising cancer rates, it's our diet, particularly the consumption of oxidising seed oils. Our skin reacts to these oils, leading to health problems.

When we connect directly with the earth walking barefoot on soil, grass or sand, we discharge excess energy. This interaction changes the body's polarity, a measurable effect that occurs through ion exchange. As you touch the ground, you're releasing built-up electrical charges into the earth, rebalancing your body's natural state. It's akin to a magnet exchanging ions with the earth, which helps ground and stabilise the body.

However, modern environments often insulate us from this natural connection. Surfaces like steel, concrete, wood, tile and asphalt block this grounding process, isolating us from the Earth's magnetic field.

There are two options: either ground yourself naturally or invest in a Pulsed Electromagnetic Field (PEMF) mat which typically costs around $5,000. While it's a significant investment, it offers a variety of benefits. When placed on your bed, the mat runs a low Gauss current, helping induce deeper sleep and making you wake up feeling more refreshed and alkaline.

PEMF mats work by pushing out electromagnetic pollution referred to as "electro smog" from sources like Wi-Fi and 5G. This technology also helps maintain the balance of your body's pH. Many people believe drinking alkaline water can shift the pH of your blood, but that is a misconception. The pH of your blood remains within a very narrow range.

However, applying a low Gauss current through the body can slightly adjust the pH and lead to a more alkaline state. An alkaline state is beneficial because it promotes disease resistance, while a more acidic state is associated with illness.

Progressive Muscle Relaxation

Another great resource for a mental health tool kit is to incorporate muscle relaxation techniques. I was introduced to this a few years ago during a stay at Ward 17. I still use muscle relaxation in everyday life. It's ten minutes out of my day and helps when used in conjunction with mindfulness and sleep hygiene. I've found trying a more holistic approach to looking after myself very beneficial.

I want you to know that understanding how the body reacts to feelings is empowering. When I was struggling with PTSD symptoms, I felt numb and couldn't understand what my body was trying to tell me. A vital connection within me felt broken, leaving me feeling vulnerable and disconnected. Whenever I experienced fear or anxiety, my body would instinctively tense up, as if bracing for impact. This physical response only deepened my discomfort, creating a cycle where emotional stress manifested in my body, and my body's tension amplified my emotional struggles.

Recognising this pattern was the first step toward healing. By practising mindfulness and learning to release tension through breathwork and self-awareness, I began to rebuild that internal connection, allowing my mind and body to work in harmony rather than conflict. This journey taught me the importance of addressing both emotional and physical responses to truly find balance and peace.

Weeks turned into months as my body ached, not from physical exercise but the constant muscle tension. Any situation can cause stress. For example, for many public speaking can be daunting and standing in front of a large audience is enough to make one's thoughts race, and the back, neck and shoulder muscles tense up. Muscle relaxation helps when anxiety is associated with muscle tension.

Even though some of those situations may not actually be dangerous, my body would respond in the same way. Sometimes, I wouldn't even notice my muscles tensing or clenching my teeth. It's also associated with backaches and tension headaches.

Progressive muscle relaxation is broken down into a few simple steps.

Set aside some time around 10 to 15 minutes and use a place for relaxation. Slow down your breathing and give yourself permission to relax.

When ready to begin, tense the muscle group chosen. Make sure you can feel the tension, but not so much that you feel a great deal of pain. Keep the muscle tensed for approximately 5 seconds, then relax the muscles and keep it relaxed for approximately 10 seconds. When you have finished the muscle relaxation, remain seated for lying down or a few moments allowing yourself to become alert.

1. Right hand and forearm. Make a fist with your right hand.
2. Right upper arm. Bring your right forearm up to your shoulder to "make a muscle".
3. Left hand and forearm.
4. Left upper arm.
5. Forehead. Raise your eyebrows as high as they will go, as though you are surprised by something.
6. Eyes and cheeks. Squeeze your eyes tight shut.
7. Mouth and jaw. Open your mouth as wide as you can as you might when you are yawning.
8. Neck. Be careful as you tense these muscles. Face forward and then pull your head back slowly as though you are looking up at the ceiling.

9. Shoulders. Tense the muscles in your shoulders as you bring your shoulders up towards your ears.
10. Shoulder blades. Push your shoulder blades back as if you want to bring them together and your chest is pushed forward.
11. Chest and stomach. Breathe in deeply, filling up your lungs.
12. Hips and buttocks. Squeeze your buttock muscles.
13. Right upper leg. Tighten your right thigh.
14. Right lower leg. Do this slowly and carefully to avoid cramps. Pull your toes towards you to stretch the calf muscle.
15. Right foot. Curl your toes downwards.
16. Left upper leg. Repeat as for the right upper leg.
17. Left lower leg. Repeat as for the right lower leg.
18. Left foot. Repeat as for the right foot.

Breathwork

Breathwork helps deepen relaxation and improve my mood. Breathing typically occurs without any thought. It's a part of normal functioning, but if I concentrate on my breathing it allows me to be in better control of my physical and mental health.

One advanced method, based on Dr Otto Warburg's research, is called multi-step oxygen therapy (MSOT), where oxygen is concentrated and breathed during exercise. Using an oxygen concentrator, a bag is filled with 900 L of 95% oxygen which is then inhaled while active, such as walking on a treadmill.

This technique increases oxygen flow, helping the body become more efficient at using oxygen to improve health.

However, not everyone has access to such equipment, but that doesn't mean the benefits of improved respiration can't be achieved.

Simple breathwork exercises can make a significant impact. For example, engaging the auxiliary muscles of respiration like the diaphragm and intercostal muscles between the ribs helps push oxygen deeper into the lungs. Over time, as posture collapses and CO_2 levels rise, many people breathe more shallowly, which can accelerate ageing. Proper breathwork reverses this trend, ensuring oxygen reaches the deepest parts of the lungs and enters the bloodstream more effectively.

One practical approach to breathwork is the Wim Hof method, involving three rounds of 30 deep breaths followed by extended breath holds. This style of breathing improves oxygen circulation and mental clarity.

An important aspect of any wellness practice is keeping small promises to yourself. These micro-commitments like going to bed at a set time, working out in the morning or even taking a moment to do breathwork are key to building a good habit, consistency, reliability and self-confidence.

My morning routine of grounding and breathwork emphasises the power of consistency, preparing my body and mind for the day ahead. This adaptable practice provides stability and mental clarity, anchoring me amidst the shifting dynamics of travel or daily life.

Cold Water Immersion

Combining breathwork, meditation, mindfulness, and cold-water immersion has transformed my mental and physical health, improving my mood, reducing stress and enhancing sleep, all while being inspired by the love and support of an amazing woman who motivates me to grow and move forward positively.

There is plenty of research indicating the benefits of recovery, reducing inflammation, soreness and clarity of plunging into cold water.

So, when I'm either submerging my whole body or partially, it's only for two minutes. Recently, I attended a sauna in Lakes Entrance, which was breathtaking. I spent 15 minutes in a Scandinavian sauna, then walked out to a balcony to jump in the ocean for a few minutes. Repeating this cycle over an hour felt incredible. I highly recommend it to anyone who travels down that way.

Research on cold-water immersion has found evidence that it helps reduce exercise-induced muscle damage that can occur after physically challenging activities. Rapid constriction of the blood vessels due to the cold water can trigger responses in the body, such as lowering metabolic activity, changing blood flow, and activating the immune system.

Cold water immersion isn't for everyone, it takes controlled breathing and the will to sit in discomfort tolerating the coldness. I'm looking forward to doing this exercise in a snow-covered lake like Chris Hemsworth completed in the series *Limitless*.

Floatation Tanks

A flotation tank, also known as a sensory deprivation tank, is an enclosed environment containing water with a high concentration of salt. The water is heated to above normal body temperature. Like the Dead Sea between Israel and Jordan which has over 30% salt levels, the water makes it easy to float on one's back and resting the head partially underwater. A floatation tank tends to be large so that even a tall person – I am over six feet – can stretch fully without touching the roof, floor or walls.

Also, no one can hear you in the tank and vice versa as it is soundproof and it is dark inside. Sensory deprivation encourages one to be quieter, to facilitate a meditative state while floating. The Epsom salts in the solution will also help with stress relief like a normal salt bath or dip in the ocean.

This is not recommended for those who are claustrophobic.

REBT

Rational Emotive Behavioural Therapy (REBT) is an approach that focuses on managing irrational or unhealthy thoughts, emotions and behaviours.

In contrast to more passive talk therapy, REBT focuses on actions. Together with a therapist, REBT helps patients to identify and dismantle unhealthy thought patterns and behaviours.

Gestalt Therapy

Gestalt therapy is an approach to psychotherapy that helps clients focus on the present to understand what is happening in their lives at this moment, and how it makes them feel in the moment, rather than what they may assume to be happening based on experience. Along with person-centred and existential therapy, it is one of the primary forms of humanistic therapy.

The term "gestalt" is derived from a German word that means "whole" or "put together." Gestalt therapy was developed in the 1940s and 1950s by Fritz Perls, a psychiatrist and psychoanalyst, and his then-wife, psychotherapist Laura Perls, as an alternative to traditional, verbally focused psychoanalysis. Their foundational premise is that people are best thought of as entities consisting of body, mind and emotions, and best understood when viewed through their own eyes.

Tremor Work

I met an amazing person in Byron Bay this year who spoke to me about Tremor Work therapy, this was an area of recovery I knew very little about. She said we all can benefit from feeling more relaxed with a calmer mind, better sleep, healthier body, happier in our relationships, more comfortable in our skin, and at peace with our place and purpose in the world. For some people, deeper relaxation is also about recovering and performing better at work, at sports or simply being able to love and care for our family and friends better.

> Overlooked by western science until now, our human body possesses a natural shaking reflex that releases stress and tension below the level of our conscious awareness. We've all seen or experienced hands shaking when public speaking or trembling after a car accident or a shock, children vibrating with excitement or simply just shaking during yoga or Pilates or when maxing out at the gym.

> This natural reflex is not a "symptom" of stress, shock, anxiety, fear, weakness or loss of control, but one of the primary ways our body releases muscular tension, relaxes the nervous system and restores our mind and body to a calm, relaxed and balanced state. It's a natural

response you can use in as little as 5–10 minutes simply lying on the floor or even in bed at night.[31]

Tension and Trauma Release Exercises (TRE) teach you how to deliberately invoke this recovery response in a safe and controlled way. This body-based technique serves to relax and rebalance your nervous system without requiring mental focus, physical effort or the need to recall the past or talk about it. Animals naturally use it, and you can do it whenever, wherever you like.

Equine Therapy

When I was in Ward 17, I had the privilege of speaking with an equine trainer who spoke about the benefits of connecting with horses which helped break down the trauma within PTSD patients.

This type of therapy involves a counsellor working with a patient and horses which helps the individual work through their reactions to events and identify responses and behaviours. The reason horses are used for this type of therapy comes down to the nature of the animal, horses value relationships with the people they interact with and are highly perceptive, responding immediately to someone's body language.

> Horses have a highly developed level of awareness and the ability to sense their surroundings. Horses apply this level of perception and awareness in their interactions with people. They respond and give feedback to what is presented, providing a calm, respectful space for us to explore our relationships and ourselves.[32]

---

31 - TRE Australia, viewed Jan 2025, https://www.treaustralia.com/

32 - Equine Assisted Therapy Australia, viewed Jan 2025, https://equineassistedtherapyaustralia.com.au/our-approach/

Horses are also non-judgemental companions, they accept us for who we are and provide a space to just be yourself, a space to relax and feel heard and seen. Horses are great teachers; they naturally embody presence and awareness. There are several places around Australia and the world that practise equine therapy.

Safe Space Mornington

I'm a big advocate for the younger generations looking after their mental and physical health. They encounter more obstacles now than I ever did when I was their age. So, I want to share about Safe Space Mornington because it can change the direction of many lives. It was an idea created by a beautiful man Matt Fontaine. As I've often said, there are people who come into our lives and leave us in awe. He is one of those rare individuals with an extraordinary gift for connecting and relating to others in a way that is both genuine and deeply empathetic. His ability to adapt and truly see the people in his community has left a profound impact on everyone who has crossed paths with him at Safe Space Mornington. It's a privilege to witness the kindness and authenticity he brings to every interaction.

This mental health support group is a wonderful idea that started in early 2024. It has allowed many members of the community young and old to attend a space without judgement or fear, where people can be themselves. This space is open to discussing any topic that relates to wellbeing, mental health gathering knowledge, and building amazing relationships and connections.

I really connected with this place and it should be modelled around Australia, to see how lives are changing every week, from the people who first thought they weren't worthy enough to now conquering the world and pushing forward to achieve their dreams.

Safe Space has become a sanctuary for many people. Matt LaFontaine's journey is as inspiring as the group he founded. Growing up in Langwarrin and Frankston and now residing in Mornington, Matt once dreamed of becoming a firefighter. For years, footy was a big part of his identity. However, this year, he decided to step away from the sport to focus on himself and his newfound passion: mental health advocacy.

Matt now dedicates his time to physical challenges and community service, helping others who are navigating mental health struggles. During the COVID-19 lockdowns in 2020 and 2021, Matt's mental health took a severe downturn. Isolation and the inability to engage in his usual activities left him feeling deeply lonely, depressed and anxious.

He found himself trapped in a cycle of playing video games for hours and consuming alcohol as a coping mechanism, which only worsened his mental state.

In June 2021, Matt hit rock bottom. One night, while out with friends, he received a seemingly trivial message that triggered a complete emotional breakdown. "I quietly left the group, intending to end my life," Matt recalls. "As I walked away in tears, my friends noticed I was gone and followed me. They intervened just in time." This life-saving intervention opened the door for Matt to seek help, not only from professionals but also from his friends and family. With time, Matt learned to open up about his struggles.

Through therapy and support from those around him, he gradually reclaimed his identity and found his way back to happiness. This personal transformation inspired him to create Safe Space, where others could also find support, community and opportunities for personal growth. Safe Space offers a welcoming environment, free of judgement, where people can share their experiences and connect with others who understand their struggles.

Recognising that mental health care can be intimidating and expensive, Matt designed Safe Space as an accessible, barrier-free option for those who may not feel comfortable talking to family or friends or who cannot afford professional help.

The world has endless possibilities, and I can add as many things as possible to my mental and physical health toolbox, but you may ask yourself, *How can I encourage someone to be open to suggestions about helping themselves?*

It's essential to empower them to make their own decisions while ensuring they feel a sense of ownership in their journey, rather than feeling directed or instructed. It's about how we strive to inspire those around us our family, friends, and colleagues. Reflecting on my own journey, there were times when I felt stuck, overwhelmed and weighed down by stress. During one of those moments, I agreed to meet with a family friend, someone who left a lasting mark on my life. His name was Alan Kearon, and though he's no longer with us, I often feel his presence, like he's sitting on my shoulder, guiding me still.

Alan was one of the most incredible and unique individuals I've ever met. I had the privilege of knowing him since I was a young boy, and over the past decade, when life felt especially heavy, he became a source of inspiration and strength. A former Victorian Police member, Alan faced his own demons, yet he carried a rare ability to connect with others on a deeply personal level. We shared a special bond, offering understanding and encouragement when I needed it most. His impact on my life continues to resonate, filling me with admiration and respect, as well as a profound sense of loss for a man who gave so much of himself to others.

Coffee catch-ups with this legend, Alan Kearon, a former Victorian Police Officer, were truly special moments in my life. His guidance was invaluable and he is terribly missed.

We would meet for coffee every couple of weeks and check in about life, he would always say, "What's happening? How are you going?" He was never one to discuss what he was dealing with first. Alan had cancer and it eventually took him. I would sit there and talk about what was happening in my life which couldn't compare to what he was feeling It gave me great strength in our conversations, and I wish he was still walking around today to see how amazing his presence was on everyone, especially his family.

I was doubtful that our conversations would change anything, but it was a way to get things off my chest. After all, I'd been struggling with this dreaded journey for years, so what difference could he possibly make in an hour over a coffee?

Alan did not offer me any advice, he did not try to challenge my thinking, and he did not attempt to persuade me of anything. And yet, within no more than five or ten minutes, I started to feel calm, centred and present. Somehow, the confusion and shame that was holding me back disappeared. Just some simple guidance transformed me into a strong, insightful, courageous person. After every conversation, I started to see my problems in a new light, not worrying about things that weren't in my control. Although my circumstances had not changed, my perspective certainly had.

If I can leave a positive impact on someone to feel inspired, that's all I need to do. Alan had that effect, and I continue to replicate this every day. It's not the temporary emotional high that I might get when someone tells me they believe in me. This was a deep sense of clarity and trust that told me that I was in the perfect place to take the next step, whatever that might be and I wasn't alone. Reflecting on conversations I had, I identified five things that anyone can consider adopting in conversations.

I can't control my mood if my mind is elsewhere, being present is essential. To use a smartphone analogy, it's like having just one app open on your screen at a time, rather than juggling multiple at once. In a world where focus and attention are increasingly rare, being fully present can transform the way you connect with and inspire those around you. When I feel like someone is judging me or analysing what I'm saying with a critical lens, it can unconsciously influence me to edit my words.

In any case, if I was having a conversation with a family member, the connection would unfold naturally, free from any agenda, opinions or judgements. This created a space where the other person felt truly safe, allowing them to think openly and clearly in a way they hadn't experienced with anyone else.

Despite having the advantage of decades of life experience, I try not to impose my own life experience on others. I must remain curious, asking occasional questions to help me explore and expand my perceptions.

I know many people who are natural problem-solvers. When someone's in trouble, it's all too easy to dish out advice without considering the longer-term impact. But giving advice, especially when someone hasn't asked for it, can unintentionally undermine them and erode their confidence to make wise decisions for themselves. Instead, it can be helpful to ask questions that enable them to connect with their own resourcefulness.

The one thing that many people struggle with is seeing the best in people. It can be hard to inspire others when losing sight of their ability to learn and grow. Instead of fixing, I remind myself of their capacity to learn. By adopting a growth mindset, I acknowledge where they are and choose to trust in their ability to get to where they like to be. Self-discovery is an amazing tool; it just takes some people longer to see the benefits of identifying all the options.

Conclusion

Bodhi: the knowledge or wisdom or awakened intellect
of a Buddha.

I contemplated how to articulate the idea of a conclusion in my book. It felt unsatisfactory to label it as an ending; rather, it signifies a new beginning. For some, this marks the start of their journey, while for others, it serves as an awakening to a realm of limitless possibilities. If I reflected on my journey, never in my wildest dreams would I have thought that writing a book would be on my bucket list.

I now understand that I was supposed to be tested on how resilient a human should be in navigating the obstacles of life, both good and bad. I'm drawn to people who have similar values and characteristics, seeing the strength in people who sit in the uncomfortable silence and rise like a phoenix out of the darkness showing a beacon of light for others to follow in their steps to live a full and positive life.

Life wasn't meant to be fair or easy. There's something that can be said about enduring tremendous stress in an event, to witness one's own inner strength. I don't know why I had the privilege to fall down with a mental health injury. Sometimes, bad things happen to good people, but I also believe things happen for a reason. I was oblivious to individual mental health. My mindset was that it would never happen to me. My physical strength was more essential than contemplating the importance of mental health.

My life today is complex with many moving parts. Now I plan special activities for just me, not because I'm selfish but because I need to look after myself before I can look after anyone else. My body and mind are required to get me to the unknown finish line. It takes commitment, effort, desire and setting goals to achieve a quality of thoughts over poor quantity to get the most out of my life and to share the untapped adventures that are waiting to be explored.

I truly enjoy the conversations with friends and colleagues about the importance of looking after personal health. If I hadn't endured the experience of the last ten years, then I would have missed the critical parts of the other person's views and feelings in most conversations. There are points in my life that I was drawn to and needed to do something about. Communicating with empathy, trust, respect and humility is the path I follow. I've made many mistakes in my life by failing what I previously attempted to achieve, I learned and continue to learn.

That's how I gain knowledge and insight into the most important person on this planet who I'm dedicated to loving the most: me. Pursuing this calling is important for my self-growth. I want to love that special person in my life unconditionally, to be there for the memorable moments and to share the days when a little comfort is needed. I will not just sit idly by and wait for something to happen; I will passionately drive toward a goal I want to reach. In the past, my belief compared this to winning a race and receiving a medal, but I forgot about the journey, the learning, the training, the failure and the success.

I've come a long way, and I hope others realise that it can be done. I've used the analogy of walking on the beach in bare feet, enjoying the cool breeze and the warmth of the sun, looking backwards over my shoulder and seeing my footprints in the sand – always moving forward but observing what I've left behind. We can't remain stagnant in life, we need to look forward and observe the sand in front of us with no footprints.

My future hasn't been written yet, the journey is unknown and exciting. The possibilities are endless with the desire to continue to grow as a person, to expand my knowledge wherever this path will take me.

Dedicating myself to hard work and breaking past my boundaries will help me push myself even further later on. If I can inspire just one person by reading this book, I've achieved what I set out to do. Having conversations with people being kind and genuine or helping them when it's not solicited can change someone's day immensely.

When I feel that someone has seen me and has taken notice that I exist, I feel important and worthy. Passing that feeling forward is easy, from opening a door for a stranger to simply smiling at someone never wanting anything in return. If we were all just a little kinder and more compassionate, life would be a lot more prosperous.

I possess experience like most people in the world, some will think the main reference is to a mental health injury but I don't see it that way. I bring both lived experience and professional expertise, yet many organisations unintentionally categorise people with lived experience in ways that create a new form of stigma.

The narrative needs to be changed on how these incredibly intelligent people are given the credibility of what they bring to the table. Having lived experience gives me a greater understanding of the complex issues that are systemic but lived experience is only a small part of someone's resume, many in the community have an abundance of knowledge and life skills which tend to be disregarded.

I've gained unique insights through experiences no one should have to endure, and I use these to help others facing similar challenges. Life's true purpose is self-development, and while no one owes me anything, I owe it to myself to keep growing. Joining the Northern Territory Police in 2004 was driven by a desire to help, protect, and educate others a passion that still drives me today.

I once believed I could navigate my career without harm, and though I was never physically struck, I faced battles with PTSD, depression and anxiety. These challenges reshaped my journey, helping me forge lifelong connections with people who resonate with my story. Their understanding isn't rooted in pity but shared experiences, reinforcing the power of authenticity and community in healing and growth.

We are all striving for better outcomes in an attempt to protect the next person who wants to follow a similar path: building resilience to life's stressors, dealing with traumatic events, looking after individual mental health and being aware of compassion fatigue and the absorption of anything and everything that affects a human being.

I want the people who come into my life to obtain a fresh perspective on personal growth; I'll consider this my small victory. When the mindset shifts to openness and a willingness to try new approaches for personal growth, it creates space for true evolution. This openness enhances self-awareness, builds confidence, and refines my intentions. Over time, this transformation of the mind begins to positively influence my physical health and the reality around me, fostering a more holistic and balanced approach to wellbeing. Over the past five years, I've noticed things have started to happen, I'm connecting with the right people at the times I never thought possible and there in my life for a reason.

The benefit of having a career in such diverse areas of Australia has given me a better understanding of the importance of who I am. For many years, I struggled with my identity after my policing career was over, no longer knowing what my purpose was anymore or the direction I was heading. Understand that in every conversation, always listen more and talk less, quiet moves are still moves. It has taken a lot of trial and error, but I will always continue to work on myself. Any change is gradual, inch by inch which then becomes steps. I celebrate the accomplishments however small they may be.

In *Way of the Peaceful Warrior* by Dan Millman, the character Socrates said, "The secret of change is to focus all of your energy, not fighting the old, but on building the new."

Maybe right now, wherever you may be, you're alone because whatever you need to learn about yourself can only be learned in solitude.

Feeling stuck often stems from the internal battle between what you think you should do and what you truly need. Sometimes, you try to force yourself to remain still, thinking that's the right solution. But deep down, there's a voice urging you to keep moving forward. It's about understanding that progress isn't always linear. Sometimes, it's the act of moving, even when it feels impossible, that leads to growth.

Feeling lost is unsettling, especially when it's paired with the chance to choose something greater than you ever imagined possible. It's the discomfort of stepping out of familiar territory and into the unknown, leaving behind the safety of what you once assumed was the best you could have. The apprehension lies in questioning whether you're ready or capable of embracing this new opportunity. However, this feeling also carries a powerful message it's not about being lost but about redefining your path and choosing to reach for something extraordinary, even when it's outside your comfort zone.

These feelings of unworthiness, being stuck and lost are deeply human and often interwoven into our personal growth journeys. They challenge us to confront our fears, embrace our vulnerabilities, and take bold steps toward becoming the best version of ourselves. Each one, when faced with courage and self-compassion, can lead to profound transformation and a deeper connection with both ourselves and others.

It's hard being open to everything, to seeing oneself through kinder eyes and giving oneself the benefit of the doubt. I recognise how far I've come over the years and give credit for those achievements. Life is trying to show me how to take care of the person I want to be. Maybe things just happened as they needed to, even if I didn't understand their sequence or reason. Embracing the discomfort, I focused on taking each day or sometimes even each hour as it came, allowing myself to fully experience what was unfolding.

The one constant that has always been present in my life is perseverance. The desire to improve self-development and gather knowledge about anything that came across my path. Roughly speaking, a worldview is a product of the synthesis between the perception of reality and the ability to shape it through action. Accordingly, we may define the process of self-development as a series of consistent iterations on the belief system to fine-tune the way one perceives the world and himself, along with a simultaneous expansion of the zone in which one is able to confidently operate. When adversity strikes, and it will, you should have several things in mind.

The first thing I had to overcome was to let go of my expectations. It's like going to my favourite coffee shop and they change the blend of the coffee. It's ok but not what I was expecting, those unfortunate things are sometimes out of my control. Even when I had everything planned out, things changed. Accepting change is hard, but it's necessary in the face of adversity. That knowledge has increased my resilience or identified it was already inside of me.

I uncovered some flaws that weren't clear for many years. I had to stand back and look at myself from a distance and stop making excuses for what happened to me. I've always thought that sometimes you have to go through the shit, to smell the fresh roses. Many organisations should do a lot better in providing support and resources for their people but ultimately everyone including myself needs to be critically invested in mental and physical health.

When I looked at my recovery, re-training my mind to view situations, experiences or obstacles when they arose, I began talking to myself, seeing three steps ahead of the dilemma I was facing. I positively told myself, *This is not life or death, take a breath. Look at what you're facing and identify some options or possibilities to solve strategically.* Practising this became a daily habit like mindfulness, exercising, meditation and scheduling short breaks throughout my day. To achieve this prepared my body for overcoming any challenges around the corner.

There are two qualities that will take me anywhere I wish to go: consistency and relentlessness. Be relentless with yourself.

I can't wrap myself or my children up in cotton wool trying to avoid disappointments or hardships of this life because I simply can't. I instead choose those uncomfortable moments, I identify my ambitions and potential obstacles, and I now stand back to think about how my legacy will leave a mark in this world. Rumination about lost opportunities only takes up space in my head which will prevent the great opportunities from appearing.

Seeing the worst in a human being to uncover the best qualities was an everyday experience throughout my career. When I started my career, I knew some things about the world. I thought I possessed a great grasp of the values of people. There were countless times I couldn't even comprehend what I observed and made a conscious decision to never put them in this book. If there is something to get out of my journey, then it is to love yourself. Invest and make time for the most important person: you. Don't just sit back and watch the world pass by, go out and take it, the world has endless opportunities to assist in making something wonderful and achievable.

We are not alone. Some days we may feel like there is no one who understands but be open and vulnerable to having conversations with another person.

There is always potential to change their life but most importantly, the possibility of changing your individual trajectory will be evident as well. The best ever project you will ever work on in life is you. You have so much colossal potential. Choose wisely and live the life that has always been yours.

While people and communities can do a lot to build resilience and support each other, real change also needs to happen at a bigger level. The Australian government hasn't done enough to tackle the mental health and social challenges many of us face. Even though awareness is growing, the policies and funding often miss the mark, leaving too many people without the help they need. It's time for the government to step up and take real action by creating programs that go to the heart of mental health issues, making support easier to access, and building spaces where empathy and connection can truly thrive. Progress means having leaders who genuinely care about the wellbeing of all Australians and are committed to creating a society where everyone has the chance to heal, grow and live well.

Bibliography

Barlow DH, Farchione TJ, Bullis JR, Gallagher MW, Murray-Latin H, Sauer-Zavala S, Bentley KH, Thompson-Hollands J, Conklin LR, Boswell JF, Ametaj A, Carl JR, Boettcher HT, Cassiello-Robbins C. "The Unified Protocol for Transdiagnostic Treatment of Emotional Disorders Compared With Diagnosis-Specific Protocols for Anxiety Disorders: A Randomized Clinical Trial" *JAMA Psychiatry*. 2017 Sep 1;74(9):875-884. doi: 10.1001/jamapsychiatry.2017.2164

Barlow DH, Sauer-Zavala S, Farchione TJ, Murray-Latin H, Ellard KK, Bullis JR, Bentley KH, Boettcher HT, Cassiello-Robbins C. *Unified Protocol for Transdiagnostic Treatment of Emotional Disorders. Workbook*. 2nd Edition. Oxford University Press, 2017.

Bergen-Cico D. "The impact of post-traumatic stress on first responders: analysis of cortisol, anxiety, depression, sleep impairment and pain" *International Paramedic Practice*. 2015 Dec;5:3. doi: 10.12968/ippr.2015.5.3.78

Beyond Blue, 2018 Nov 29, "Answering the call national survey: National Mental Health and Wellbeing Study of Police and Emergency Services – Final report." https://apo.org.au/node/206886

Black Dog Institute, "Transcranial Magnetic Stimulation (TMS) treatment for depression", viewed Jan 2025, https://www.blackdoginstitute.org.au/research-centres/neuromodulation-research-centre/transcranial-magnetic-stimulation-tms/

"Gary Brecka's Recommended Salt | Baha Gold Sea Salt", 2024 Mar 7, YouTube, Brecka G. https://www.youtube.com/watch?v=mAaSgTMK85w

Chevalier G, Sinatra ST, Oschman JL, Delany RM. "Earthing (grounding) the human body reduces blood viscosity-a major factor in cardiovascular disease" *J Altern Complement Med.* 2013 Feb;19(2):102-10. doi: 10.1089/acm.2011.0820

Cleveland Clinic, "Autonomic Nervous System", viewed Jan 2025, https://my.clevelandclinic.org/health/body/23273-autonomic-nervous-system

Cunov K. "The Difference Between Pleasure, Sensual, Sexual & Erotic – and Why It Matters", 2020 Dec 22. https://kendracunov.com/2020/12/22/the-difference-between-pleasure-sensual-sexual-erotic-and-why-it-matters/

Davis DM, Hayes JA. "What are the benefits of mindfulness? A practice review of psychotherapy-related research" *Psychotherapy (Chic).* 2011 Jun;48(2):198-208. doi: 10.1037/a0022062

Davis DM, Hayes JA. "What are the benefits of mindfulness?" *Monitor on Psychology.* 2012 Jul 1;43(7). https://www.apa.org/monitor/2012/07-08/ce-corner

Eldredge J. *Wild at Heart: Discovering the Secret of a Man's Soul.* Thomas Nelson, 2001.

Equine Assisted Therapy Australia, viewed Jan 2025, https://equineassistedtherapyaustralia.com.au/our-approach/

Fisher H. *Why We Love: The Nature and Chemistry of Romantic Love.* Henry Holt and Company, 2004.

Food Standards Australia New Zealand (FSANZ), "How much sodium do Australians eat?", viewed Jan 2025, https://www.foodstandards.gov.au/consumer/nutrition/sodium-salt/salthowmuch

Foss K. "What is Toxic Masculinity and How it Impacts Mental Health" *Anxiety & Depression Association of America*. 2022 Nov 14. https://adaa.org/learn-from-us/from-the-experts/blog-posts/consumer/what-toxic-masculinity-and-how-it-impacts-mental

Healthline, "A Beginner's Guide to the 7 Chakras and Their Meanings", viewed Jan 2025, https://www.healthline.com/health/fitness-exercise/7-chakras

Healthy Minds, "What is dissociation?", viewed Jan 2025, https://www.healthyminds.services/support/articles/dissociation

HyperPhysics (Georgia State University), "Gauss's Law", viewed Jan 2025, http://hyperphysics.phy-astr.gsu.edu/hbase/electric/gaulaw.html

Kanakis K & McShane C. "Preparing for disaster: preparedness in a flood and cyclone prone community" *Australian Journal of Emergency Management*. 2016 April;31:2. https://knowledge.aidr.org.au/resources/ajem-apr-2016-preparing-for-disaster-preparedness-in-a-flood-and-cyclone-prone-community/

Kang Y, Strecher VJ, Kim E, Falk EB. "Purpose in life and conflict-related neural responses during health decision-making" *Health Psychol*. 2019;38, 545–552. doi: 10.1037/hea0000729

Kim ES, Strecher VJ, Ryff CD. "Purpose in life and use of preventive health care services" *Proc. Natl. Acad. Sci*. 2014;111, 16331–16336. doi: 10.1073/pnas.1414826111

Koziol C. "Journaling's Impact on Mental Health" UWL *Journal of Undergraduate Research XXIV*. 2021. https://www.uwlax.edu/globalassets/offices-services/urc/jur-online/pdf/2021/koziol.callie.eng.pdf

Kyron MJ, Rikkers W, Bartlett J, Renehan E, Hafekost K, Baigent M, Lawrence D. "Mental health and wellbeing of Australian police and emergency services employees" *Archives of Environmental & Occupational Health*. 2021;77(4), pp. 282–292. doi: 10.1080/19338244.2021.1893631

LeWine HE. "Sexual side effects of SSRIs: Why it happens and what to do Coping with this common side effect from antidepressants" *Havard Health Publishing*. 2023 Jul 7. https://www.health.harvard.edu/womens-health/when-an-ssri-medication-impacts-your-sex-life

Maglione MA, Chen C, Bialas A, Motala A, Chang J, Akinniranye G, Hempel S. "Stress Control for Military, Law Enforcement, and First Responders: A Systematic Review" *Rand Health Q*. 2022 Jun 30;9(3):20. https://pmc.ncbi.nlm.nih.gov/articles/PMC9242555/

Mayo Clinic, May 2024, "Electroconvulsive therapy (ECT)", viewed Jan 2025, https://www.mayoclinic.org/tests-procedures/electroconvulsive-therapy/about/pac-20393894

Millman D. *Way of the Peaceful Warrior*. JP Tarcher, 1980.

Moore C. "Positive Daily Affirmations: Is There Science Behind It?" *Optimism & Mindset*. 2019 Mar 4. https://positivepsychology.com/daily-affirmations/

Oschman JL, Chevalier G, Brown R. "The effects of grounding (earthing) on inflammation, the immune response, wound healing, and prevention and treatment of chronic inflammatory and autoimmune diseases" *J Inflamm Res*. 2015 Mar 24;8:83-96. doi: 10.2147/JIR.S69656

Paiva-Salisbury ML & Schwanz KA. "Building Compassion Fatigue Resilience: Awareness, Prevention, and Intervention for Pre-Professionals and Current Practitioners" *J Health Serv. Psychol*. 2022;48(1):39-46. doi: 10.1007/s42843-022-00054-9

"Don't Underestimate The Hole Your Absence Would Leave", 2024 Aug 19, YouTube, Peterson J. https://www.youtube.com/watch?v=kEWD8m3hVbk

Pilar Matud M. "Gender differences in stress and coping styles" 2004;37:7. doi: 10.1016/j.paid.2004.01.010

Police Federation of Australia 2022, "Police Federation of Australia submission to the Employment White Paper" PFA, Canberra. https://pfa.org.au/wp-content/uploads/2023/01/20221130_PFA-Submission_Employment-White-Paper.pdf

Psychology Today, "Love and Sex", viewed Jan 2025, https://www.psychologytoday.com/intl/basics/relationships/love-and-sex

Riès SK, Dronkers NF, Knight RT. "Choosing words: left hemisphere, right hemisphere, or both? Perspective on the lateralization of word retrieval" *Ann NY Acad Sci.* 2016 Apr;1369(1):111-31. doi: 10.1111/nyas.12993

Roussos E. "Former NT Police officer calls for an overhaul of mental health services following recent suicides", *ABC News*, 2022 May 12. https://www.abc.net.au/news/2022-05-12/northern-territory-police-mental-health-suicide/101038706

Schippers MC & Ziegler N. "Life Crafting as a Way to Find Purpose and Meaning in Life" *Front Psychol.* 2019 Dec 13;10:2778. doi: 10.3389/fpsyg.2019.02778

Senate Standing Committees on Education and Employment 2019, *The people behind 000: mental health of our first responders*, SSCEE, Canberra.

Sinatra ST, Sinatra DS, Sinatra SW, Chevalier G. "Grounding – The universal anti-inflammatory remedy" *Biomed J.* 2023 Feb;46(1):11-16. doi: 10.1016/j.bj.2022.12.002

Smyth JM, Johnson JA, Auer BJ, Lehman E, Talamo G, Sciamanna CN. "Online Positive Affect Journaling in the Improvement of Mental Distress and Well-Being in General Medical Patients With Elevated Anxiety Symptoms: A Preliminary Randomized Controlled Trial" *JMIR Ment Health.* 2018 Dec 10;5(4):e11290. doi: 10.2196/11290

Stileman HM & Jones CA. "Revisiting the debriefing debate: does psychological debriefing reduce PTSD symptomology following work-related trauma? A meta-analysis" *Front Psychol.* 2023 Dec 21;14:1248924. doi: 10.3389/fpsyg.2023.1248924

TRE Australia, viewed Jan 2025, https://www.treaustralia.com/

Verma R et al. "Gender differences in stress response: Role of developmental and biological determinants" *Industrial Psychiatry Journal.* Jan–Jun 2011;20(1):p 4-10. doi: 10.4103/0972-6748.98407

Violanti JM, Charles LE, McCanlies E, Hartley TA, Baughman P, Andrew ME, Fekedulegn D, Ma CC, Mnatsakanova A, Burchfiel CM. "Police stressors and health: a state-of-the-art review" *Policing.* 2017 Nov;40(4):642-656. doi: 10.1108/PIJPSM-06-2016-0097

WHO, 2023, "Depressive disorder (depression)", viewed Jan 2025, https://www.who.int/news-room/fact-sheets/detail/depression

Wright P. "Men tend to regulate their emotions through actions rather than words" *The Centre for Male Psychology.* 2023 Aug 1. https://www.centreformalepsychology.com/male-psychology-magazine-listings/men-tend-to-regulate-their-emotions-through-actions-rather-than-words

List of Images

1. Uluru, NT: heart of our beautiful nation I fell in love with.
2. New police recruits. (PFES College Darwin)
3. Alice Springs: a beautiful desert town by day and in recent years a dangerous place at night.
4. Alice Springs Police Station: a place of amazing people, fun times and a memory of the worst incidents in human nature.
5. Car Crash Humpty Doo: the driver escaped on foot from the scene.
6. Car Crash Humpty Doo: amazing no one was hurt.
7. South of Alice Springs, 2012, before my world was turned upside down.
8. Big O at Titjikala, NT: maintaining the connections over the years is important.
9. Losing my identity was a terrible stage in my life, no direction and no purpose.
10. Finding new purpose and direction, always moving forward.
11. Coming out of the shadows to begin my advocacy work for first responders.
12. Heart2Heart Walk media conference at the National Police Memorial. (Canberra, ACT)

13. Heart2Heart Walk media conference at the National Police Memorial. (Canberra, ACT)

14. Physical fitness and mental fitness are entwined together.

15. Be open to trying new ways of looking after my mental and physical health. (Mills Beach, Mornington Peninsula, VIC)

16. I draw my energy from nature, the beach is my happy place. (Mills Beach, Mornington Peninsula, VIC)

17. A-Watch Alice Springs Patrol group: what a team, what a crazy rewarding experience.

18. Finke Desert Race 2012, Prologue Day ... can't see I'm nervous at all.

19. Building connections and relationships are important professionally and personally; with the Chief Minister of the NT, Hon Lia Finocchiaro (right) at the Parliament House. (Darwin, NT)

20. Finding the most rewarding connection unexpectedly, a very special moment in my life. (Toorak College Ball, Melbourne, VIC)

21. The most amazing woman in the world: there aren't enough words in existence to describe how beautiful she is.

22. Leaving footprints in the sand: reflecting how far I've come on my journey. (Lakes Entrance, VIC)

23. Coffee catch-ups with this legend, Alan Kearon, a former Victorian Police Officer, were truly special moments in my life. His guidance was invaluable and he is terribly missed.

24. Back Cover: Paul Milne.

Testimonials

As a clinical psychologist with over three decades of experience, I have had the privilege of working with individuals whose professions expose them to significant trauma and adversity. These include those working in policing, emergency services and the military. In my experience, these individuals are often altruistic by nature. They are drawn to careers that allow them to serve their communities, work as part of a team and contribute to something meaningful. Most can readily recall personal and professional highlights from their careers.

Typically joining these professions in their late teens or early twenties, few consider the long-term impacts their work might have on their psychological and physical health, as well as their personal relationships. While most organisations now offer programs designed to help individuals build and maintain psychological resilience, this has not always been the case. Even today, it can be difficult to encourage early-career professionals to consistently engage in protective or preventative practices. And even when they do, it is impossible to completely avoid trauma exposure and its associated effects.

This is why relatable personal stories – of lived experiences with trauma and adversity, as well as successful recovery – are so powerful. These stories can inspire hope, reduce stigma, and provide valuable insights for others who may be struggling.

I first met Paul in 2023 while he was organising a long-distance charity walk to raise awareness about first responders' mental health and wellbeing. We quickly discovered a shared passion for increasing awareness around the challenges faced by those in high-risk occupations, as well as reducing the barriers, both real and perceived, to seeking help. I was deeply impressed by Paul's commitment to advocacy and his ability to galvanize support from across different agencies, the community and political leaders.

In this book, Paul demonstrates tremendous insight, courage and vulnerability as he shares his deeply personal journey. His transition from being a mature, successful and dedicated police officer to feeling isolated, unable to function and suicidal will resonate with many – whether through their own experiences or those of colleagues or loved ones. Paul does not shy away from describing his raw emotions: confusion, fear, anger, shame, feelings of betrayal by his organisation, and the deterioration of relationships with colleagues, friends, leaders and ultimately his family.

Crucially, Paul also shares his journey of recovery. He documents the significant challenges he faced in asking for help – a daunting step for many – and navigating the reality of being diagnosed with mental health conditions. He candidly describes his struggle to find effective treatments and therapists who could assist him and emphasises the ongoing effort required to maintain his health and wellbeing.

Paul's reflections go beyond his personal story; he highlights opportunities for prevention or earlier intervention at key points in his career. He identifies areas where improvements could be made at systemic, team, leadership and individual levels. Drawing on both lived experience and research, he offers practical suggestions for changes in training, organisational support systems, and supervision practices. Importantly, Paul also examines what he could have done differently – a powerful approach that ensures this book is not only relatable but also actionable.

This book is an invaluable resource for individuals working in high-risk sectors who want to safeguard their health and wellbeing throughout their careers. It is equally relevant for leaders seeking to create supportive environments for their teams. Moreover, Paul's insights will resonate with the loved ones of those in these professions, helping them better understand the challenges faced by their partners, family members or friends.

Paul deserves immense credit for using his experiences, and his persistence and resilience, to create something that will undoubtedly assist others. His aim is clear: to give hope to those who may face similar struggles. I am confident that many readers will find that hope within these pages.

– Nicole Sadler AM, CSC
Professor Director and CEO, Phoenix Australia – Centre for Posttraumatic Mental Health, Department of Psychiatry, University of Melbourne

•

"Through persistence, inspiration and resilience, I never gave up on life. My journey is to give you hope that you too can do this when required."

Paul shares his raw and powerful insight into his mental health journey – a journey that can only be described as remarkable and inspiring.

Having worked as a police officer, he faced unimaginable challenges that ultimately led to his PTSD. When he first started therapy with me, he was merely a shadow of the man he is today. He struggled to be present, weighed down by numbness, catastrophic thinking, self-judgemental, and riddled with anger. Sleep was elusive, he was haunted by vivid and relentless traumatic dreams.

But through sheer determination and a willingness to confront his pain head-on, Paul refused to let PTSD define him. He worked tirelessly to reclaim his life, battling through the darkest moments to emerge stronger, more self-aware, and deeply committed to healing.

Throughout this journey, he engaged in a range of therapeutic interventions – both medical and psychological – alongside personal strategies that supported his recovery. In this book, he shares the tools that have worked for him, from evidence-based therapies to lifestyle practices such as regular ice baths, exercise, mindfulness, journaling, developing a growth mindset, engaging in healthy relationships and "growing a tool kit". These strategies have not only aided his recovery but have also reshaped his perspective on life, allowing him to enhance his resilience and life purpose.

Over the past few years, Paul's purpose has transformed. He has become a mentor, role model and advocate for first responders, dedicated to improving mental health awareness within emergency services. His impact has extended beyond his own recovery, inspiring others to seek help.

Paul dives deep into the despair of his past, openly sharing the struggles he endured and the steps he took to rebuild his life. His story is one of courage, resilience, and hope – a testament to the power of persistence and self-discovery.

I have no doubt that his journey will inspire many, offering a guiding light to those who need it most.

– **Nicole Plotkin**
Director and Principal Psychologist BA, BAppSc Psych (Hons),
GDipDisability Studies, Cert4 Workplace Training and Assessment, MAPS

•

Paul's journey is the epitome of resilience and self-awareness – proof that showing up for yourself, again and again, is what makes the difference. As I read his words, I saw so many parallels to my own journey that I could have written them myself.

This book is a gift to first responders. It's for those who might not recognise the signs of PTSD, compassion fatigue, moral injury or depression creeping in. It's for those of us who once believed we were tough enough to handle anything, only to realise the job was taking more from us than we ever expected. We signed up to help people, to make a difference, to do good in the world – only to find ourselves struggling under the weight of it all.

Paul's honesty about his own diagnosis, treatment and recovery is one of the greatest acts of kindness he could offer to his fellow first responders – those still serving, those retired, and those anywhere in between. The journey through a mental health injury can feel isolating, but Paul reminds us that we're not alone. And most importantly, he shows us that healing is possible.

Like Paul, I used to think therapy would "fix" me after a couple of sessions. But that's not how this works. Recovery isn't something that just happens to us – it's something we have to take ownership of. It wasn't until I truly accepted that I had to be an active participant in my own healing that things started to shift. Paul gets that. Throughout this book, he reminds us to be open to different approaches – to try things we might have dismissed before, to be willing to step outside our comfort zones and to give ourselves the grace to heal in a way that works for us.

One of the most powerful things Paul does in this book is call out the stigma, particularly for men, around mental health in the first responder community. In Australia, we lose an average of nine people to suicide every day – seven of them are men. That statistic alone should be enough to make us rethink how we approach mental health. Books like this help us break down those barriers, making it clear that reaching out for help isn't a weakness – it's a strength.

And beyond all of this, what really stood out to me was the way Paul talks about his partner, Vicki. The love, respect and gratitude he has for her shines through these pages. It's a reminder of just how important our relationships are, and how crucial it is that we nurture them rather than take them for granted.

Paul's dedication to his own recovery, and his willingness to share his experience, is an act of selflessness. This book isn't just words on a page – it's a lifeline, a reminder that no matter how dark things feel, there's a way forward. And that's something every first responder deserves to hear.

– Rosie Skene

Former Operational Safety Instructor, Weapons and Tactics, NSW Police Force

Founder Tactical Yoga Australia, Podcast Host, Triumph Beyond Trauma

●

After agreeing to review Paul's book, *The Urgent Connection*, I made the (incorrect) assumption that it would be a book filled with pure policing stories of Paul's time in the Northern Territory Police. As I was about to find out, it is far from it, it is more of an educational piece.

Yes, Paul delves into the rigours, the dangers, the trauma, the excitement and the "not knowing what is going to happen today" of policing with an array of various policing experiences that Paul encountered. However, *The Urgent Connection* heavily focuses on the emotional toll that policing took on Paul and this is where the beauty within this book lay, how he emerged from it.

Paul goes into detail about the heartbreak of not being able to be a proper father to his beloved children due to his mental injuries, having compassion fatigue, fighting the internal and external stigma that is so commonly attached to mental health and his inevitable diagnoses of PTSD, major depression and anxiety.

Post-diagnoses is where *The Urgent Connection* becomes an educational piece as Paul delves into how he emerged from his mental darkness and into the mentally healthy, functioning and driven person he is today.

Overcoming his strong internal and the ever-present external stigma, Paul details that once he made the decision to seek professional assistance and confront his inner demons, he opened the door to his second life, a life that is filled with a strong desire and equally strong drive to do what he needed (and continues) to do and to be mentally healthy.

Psychological treatment, diet changes, fitness regimes, meditation, mindfulness, breath work, journaling, religious and spiritual activities, and a distinctively recognised positive attitude are all documented in the book, all of which went into Paul's transformation from Paul v1 to Paul v2.

There is no simple recovery from mental injuries. I speak from experience with the same diagnoses as Paul's, you must work and work hard and maintain that hard work.

Paul found new purpose and direction, clarity of life, the love of his life, and the power of post-traumatic growth, utilising a magnitude of tools within his mental health toolbox.

This book proves that even though you may experience mental darkness, there is a path out of that darkness using the tools that Paul was introduced to and chose to use.

– Mark Thomas
Former Victorian Police Sergeant
Public Speaker, Advocate for First Responders and Veterans
Founder and President of the Code 9 Foundation

●

I met Paul in 2022 when we had both been inspired by the Heart2Heart Walk, an awareness-raising mission aiming to walk from the heart of the Nation, Lambert Centre of Australia, to the heart of the nation, Canberra, calling for action on first responders' mental health.

We found ourselves signing up to be part of the organising and planning committee as volunteers. I was immediately struck by Paul's deep sincerity and his quiet and humble way of honouring, listening and supporting the many voices, stories and experiences that were within that volunteer committee.

As I got to know Paul, I quickly realised that my observed admiration was only the beginning of the true depth of his character and person. We quickly became fast friends. Yes, it may have been a slight trauma bond as we were both experiencing and living with the impact of first responders' mental health issues, albeit from very different experiences and perspectives – Paul as the first responder and I as the wife of one.

However, I was to learn the true essence of Paul's deep kindness and incredible joy at looking forward, looking within and creating purpose from his experiences not only for himself and his deeply treasured family but also for those who are fortunate enough to be in his circle; be that a friend, colleague or someone fortunate enough to pick up this book.

Paul is acutely aware that each of us has our own path and set of circumstances in what is often a shared experience of a first responder's mental health injury. He honours that difference and offers his perspective and his story as a way to help others. By sharing his reflections and hard-fought learnings, Paul's narrative is an opportunity for others to develop their own understanding and acceptance of what they have been through but, most importantly, to also acknowledge the power and strength that they can draw from their hardships and challenges.

It's no accident that Paul has become an incredible voice for the voiceless in the first responder landscape through his considered, thoughtful, sometimes humorous and always kind and heartfelt learnings.

Before and beyond this book, Paul has graciously used his experience to highlight the importance of connection when dealing with mental health challenges but more than that, he has fearlessly raised awareness of the all-too-often silent experiences of first responders with psychological harm and injury.

For so many first responders, psychological injury is the impact of a dedicated and honourable service. This injury can have a devastating impact on every facet and aspect of an officer's life, leaving them in a space without understanding or hope. What Paul has bravely done in this book is to provide comfort, solace and recognition for all who may share a similar path as he. What so many going through this experience need is support and care, be that in the form of a doctor, colleague, family member or friend. But those connections can often be very challenging to find in these dark times and sometimes the ability to acknowledge one's own experience to safely find the needed support may not be there in the grip of the challenges.

What Paul has done with this book is to offer another opportunity for connection and give his own support, comfort and guidance to others who may be facing their own experiences and challenges of a first responder psychological injury.

I am deeply proud and honoured to know Paul and so very fortunate and grateful to call him a friend.

I encourage readers to embark on this shared experience with courage and hope, and the knowledge that through the connection of reading this story you are not alone.

– Sarah U'Brien
Recovery and Resilience Specialist
Living Alongside PTSD, Loving Partner and Mother

www.ingramcontent.com/pod-product-compliance
Lightning Source LLC
Chambersburg PA
CBHW061216070526
44584CB00029B/3857